CU00983287

Barranquilla Carnival

Contents

Welcome!

Mysterious ruins obscured by ancient rainforests. Charming colonial towns with romantic, cobblestone alleyways. Authentic, hole-in the-wall venues hosting late-night salsa parties... Welcome to Colombia, where the only risk is wanting to stay.

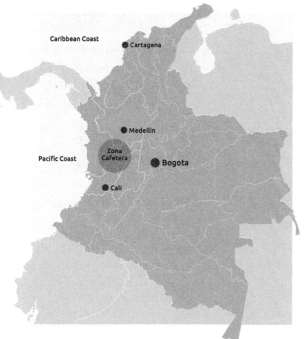

Our Insiders' Picks of Colombia's Top 10 Experiences

Immerse yourself in the Zona Cafetera

Grand adventures await in the central mountain corridors of Colombia. Home to one of the friendliest and most admired cultural demographics – the Paisas – this region is known as the Colombian Coffee Axis, or the *Eje Cafetero*.

Discover some of the best gourmet coffee shops, fine dining, and a variety of hotels, hostels, and country villas for rent in the region's capital of Pereira.

Breathe in the mountain air in the outlying areas of Pereira. Here, you'll also find bird-watching parks, hiking and mountain-biking trails, camping grounds, waterfalls, and even an exotic garden that's home to over 40,000 species of plants and lizards.

Trek the Lost City or La Ciudad Perdida

This four-to-six-day trek takes you through the jungles of the Sierra Nevada de Santa Marta and into a place of myth and legend.

Built by the Tayrona indigenous tribe

La Ciudad Perdida

some 65 years before Machu Picchu, this 3,000sqm "lost city" of mysterious stone terraces is only accessible by a 1,200-step mossy stone stairway from the Buritaca river.

Known as Teyuna to the local people, the architectural style here is unique. Only a few are said to understand the meaning behind its complex plans and many believe the jungle still hides another 9,000sqm of unexplored structures in thick growth.

Salsa the night away in Cali

Music and dance are a huge part of Colombian culture, and Cali certainly flaunts its title of "Salsa Capital of the World" with aplomb.

Attracting the finest movers and burgeoning stars, Tin Tin Deo's reputation spans the entire country. This diminutive second-floor club, its walls emblazoned with salsa icons, comes alive on weekends.

La Topa Tolondra is another popular club: it's relaxed, informal, and open virtually every day of the week, making it especially popular with travelers.

Explore Old Town Cartagena and Getsemaní

Home to many of Cartagena's most iconic architectural gems and historic sites is the exquisitely preserved Old Town.

Highlights here include the large Plaza de la Aduana – Cartagena's oldest plaza – and the Plaza San Pedro Clave. Both are perfect spots to grab a cup of Colombian coffee (or a hot-chocolate-and-cheese) at the outdoor cafes and

Cartagena

"

At sunset, climb up to the western sea-facing wall of Catagena's old town and watch the sun setting over the Caribbean.

sample the seasonal offerings of the roving fruit vendors.

At sunset, climb up to the western sea-facing wall and watch the sun setting over the Caribbean.

Afterwards, take the main road and walk towards Getsemaní. The former slave quarter has been transformed into Cartagena's most charming and authentic neighborhood – a place where seasoned travelers mingle with young backpackers and locals.

Packed with dozens of the city's hippest cafes, bars, and hotels, it's home to the some of the city's best nightlife options, and the rumba goes well into the morning.

Experience true Afro-Colombian culture in La Boquilla Fishing Village

La Boquilla is located on the outskirts of northern Cartagena on the

Gregg Bleakney

Caribbean coast, and has remained relatively untouched by tourism.

Inhabited by Afro-Colombian ethnic groups, the beaches here are lined with palm-thatched huts. Arrive at sunrise and spend time with local fishermen as they cast their nets into the water, and watch as they prepare their catch of the day for sale.

If you prefer a sleep-in, there are a variety of other activities to further explore the village and culture, too. Canoe tours through mangrove swamps, bird watching, bathing in medicinal volcanic mud, watching a traditional dance, and, of course, learning about fishing from the locals are all on the agenda.

Hike through Tayrona National Natural Park

Revel in a natural park where tropical forests embrace the Caribbean Sea. This serene paradise is home to at least 56 endangered species, but most stay out of sight, leaving you in a cacophony of monkey shrieks and bird songs.

For the fit and adventurous, enter via Calabazo and climb to the pre-Hispanic ruins of Pueblito – a once-thriving community of the Tayrona tribe. Here, the remains of more than 500 dwellings were discovered, estimated to have been home to 4,000 people at one point in history.

If you're looking to enjoy a piece of the Caribbean good life, head to Cabo San Juan. This idyllic beach is a hotspot for social young travelers. With a relaxed, easy-going atmosphere, get ready to make new friends over beers at the beach bar, or fall asleep to the sounds of the ocean breeze while on an aerial hammock.

Be part of the crowd at a football match

No trip to Colombia would be complete without experiencing the country's national pastime: football. Uniting Colombians across the nation, the sight of red or yellow t-shirts, people

Splash in the refreshing waters of the Pance River, which originates high in the Farallones de Cali.

leaving work early, and shops closing at noon are all signs that a soccer match is on that day. The largest stadium is El Metropolitano in Barranquilla – home ground of Colombia's national soccer team. Grab the face paint and don't miss a chance to experience the electric energy of a soccer match here.

Surf, dive, and relax on Guachalito Beach

If you're looking for something a little more slow-paced, don't miss the stunning Guachalito Beach, an hour by boat from Nuquí on the Pacific coast.

This isolated beach, fringed with verdant jungle, has several guesthouses, as well as some of the best humpback whale-watching and ecotourism in the region.

Divers of all abilities will be spoilt with an abundant kaleidoscope of marine life, warm tropical waters, and a wide range of diving conditions here.

If you've always wanted to try surfing, the mild currents here are perfect for beginners, too.

Marvel at a city's rebirth in Medellin's library parks

Dotted throughout Medellín, you'll find several library parks – each with their own style and architectural personality.

Built between 2008 and 2010 with support from the Spanish government, and strategically placed within the city's most marginalized communities, these parks played an instrumental role in transforming public spaces into safe, accessible, and inclusive parks for everyone.

Colombian Currency

The currency in Colombia is the Colombian Peso (COP$), which can be withdrawn from all ATMs.

Colombia is still very much a cash economy. Although most hotels and tour companies will accept credit cards, many smaller shops and restaurants won't, so always carry some cash.

Tipping is not usually expected, but fancier places will add a discretionary 10% service charge onto your bill. Some places will ask if you'd like to include service in your bill.

Bargaining in markets is common, but aggressive tactics are not welcome. Always haggle with a smile.

The most common scams involve fake banknotes. The best way to identify a real note is to hold it up to the light and check for a watermark of the person depicted on the note.

❝❞

Revel in a natural park where tropical forests embrace the Caribbean Sea.

For great views of Medellín, take a cable car ride to Santo Domingo Savio Library Park, which sits on the eastern mountain slopes.

Spend a day of adventure in Pance River

Splash in the refreshing waters of the Pance River, which originates high in the Farallones de Cali, or go running, biking, or hiking through the surrounding mountains.

This little gem is 25min from Cali, so avoid the weekends if you want some peace and quiet.

For a "fresher" experience, head up the river, where you'll encounter an ice-cold waterfall that crashes down into a natural pool.

You can also walk all the way up to Pance Village, where the locals like to bring their pots and pans on weekends and make a fire to cook *sancocho* – a chicken and vegetable soup – for a hearty lunch by the river.

Climate & Weather

Thanks to its proximity to the equator, Colombia has a mostly warm and tropical climate. However, as the country has five major climatic zones, temperatures will vary depending on the altitude and the season you're visiting in.

High travel season

Peak travel season is usually between December and February. Expect sunny days of 24°C (75°F) in the Andes and the Caribbean. On the Pacific coast, Chocó, and the Amazon, it's typically warm and humid during this time, with temperatures around 27°C (80°F).

The Amazon is driest between March-October, exposing some beautiful hiking paths and white-sand beaches.

Bogota is spring-like all year round, with cool days and crisp nights. Though it can get quite hot on sunny days.

When you're planning your visit, be aware that hotels and transport books up fast on national holidays, especially during the Christmas and Easter periods.

For the perfect combination of good weather and fewer crowds, February and March are the best times to visit.

Wet season in Colombia

Colombia suffers from both the El Niño and La Niña weather phenomenon, with many departments severely affected by water shortage and extreme rainfall.

October and November are typically low season in Colombia, with flash floods and rainy weather hitting the Andean region and the Caribbean coast.

Bogota, Medellín, and Cali suffer a second rainy season in April and May, with hard rains hitting Cartagena especially in May, so avoid traveling during this time.

Finally, June to November is hurricane season. Flooding, landslides, and torrential rains can take place.

Volcanic activity

The most active volcano is Nevado del Ruiz, in Los Nevados National Park within the Coffee Zone.

Chiles and Cerro Negro volcanoes in the department of Nariño are also on high alert, as they have shown increased activity since the earthquake that hit the area in 2014.

Before traveling to areas with known volcanic activity, take note of any official warnings and advice from local authorities.

Altitude Sickness

Bogota's high altitude of 2,640m (8,661ft) might cause some travelers to feel the effects of altitude sickness.

Symptoms include tiredness, headaches, dizziness, nausea, and shortness of breath. Within a few days, you'll feel fine as long as you stay hydrated.

Don't drink alcohol and avoid anything that requires too much exertion, like hiking or a salsa class. Just take it easy for a couple of days and allow your body to acclimatize.

What to Pack

Prepare for a variety of climates and temperatures. It's a common mistake to pack nothing but shorts and t-shirts for a tropical climate, and then find yourself freezing cold in the Andean regions.

• Always bring some warmer items of clothing – layering is the key.

• Be wary of mosquitoes. Pack some light, long-sleeved clothes and insect repellent.

• Colombians are very neat and formal people, especially in big cities, so going out to dinner in shorts and flip-flops are a no-no. Pack at least one smart-casual outfit.

Language & Phrases

Overall, English proficiency across the country is low. So, learn a few Spanish phrases to show the locals that you're trying to meet them halfway – it's not only good manners, it'll encourage them to use the little English they do know without fear of embarrassment. Don't forget that Colombians love to talk! Being able to have a basic conversation with them can culturally and socially enrich your trip, bringing you much closer to this crazy-cool culture.

Cartagena

Learning Spanish

Spanish schools and private classes are aplenty in major tourist destinations like Bogota, Medellín, the Coffee Zone, and Cartagena.

With accents varying from region to region, it's best to first learn the neutral accent of the Andean cities before you engage with the locals along the Caribbean Coast: despite the easygoing lifestyle, they talk like a gun spitting bullets, and completely swallow the letter "s".

Key Phrases for Travelers

Hello: *Hola/Buenos días*

How are you? *¿Cómo estás? /¿Todo bien?*

Goodbye: *Adiós/Chao/Hasta luego/Nos vemos*

Thank you: *Gracias*

Please: *Por favor*

Excuse me/I'm sorry: *Disculpe*

I'm X: *Soy "X"* (your name)

I'm from X: *Soy de "X"* (your Country of Residence)

Where is the "X":
En dónde está "X"
— **bathroom:** *el baño*
— **bus stop:** *paradero de bus*
— **pharmacy:** *la drogueria*

(To taxi driver) Can you please take me to "X": *Me lleve por favor hasta "X"*

I don't speak Spanish: *Yo no hablo español*

Can you repeat that more slowly? *¿Puede repetirlo más despacio?*

I would like "X": *Me gustaría "X"*

Would you please give me: *Me regala por favor "X"* (literally means, "would you gift me... ?" but is commonly used when asking for something eg. an empanada)

How much? *Cuánto cuesta?*

Thank you, but I'm waiting for my friends: *Gracias, pero estoy esperando a mis amigos*

Sorry, but I'm not interested: *Lo siento, pero no estoy interesada/o*

Cool! *¡Chevere! / ¡Bacano!*

Ready/done/ok/agree: *¡Listo!*

Party: *Rumba*

I have a terrible hangover: *Tengo un guayabo terrible*

Where to Stay

Unlike many developed countries, accommodations in Colombia don't often have an online presence, so it can be hard to make a booking. But, if you know where to look, you'll find this country is full of unique, authentic, and charming options to rest your head.

Medellín

Hotels in Colombia

Sure, Colombia hosts all the common international hotel chains, plus a slew of local ones too. But don't settle for these overstated, corporate hotels selling dusty, "in-the-box" products.

The famous local colors and charm really come to life in the niche and boutique hotels of Colombia.

Sites like Trip Advisor or a search within Facebook Groups are great ways to get the latest local recommendations. If you're already in the midst of your journey, keep an ear out for "trail talk" on recommendations

El Guyabal

from your fellow travelers – just be sure to do a little research before committing to your stay.

Hostels

When it comes to hostels in Colombia, you really need to read customer reviews carefully. You might find a hostel that looks really cool and has plenty of friendly people, but turns out to have uncomfortable beds and poorly-lit rooms.

You don't have to go to the most expensive hostel, but definitely search for ones that suit your travel style. This could be a more conservative bed and breakfast, or a social, 'meet people and party' vibe.

Always carry locks for your bags and/or lockers – especially if you're staying in a group dorm. Try to keep your stuff well-organized to prevent accidental loss or theft.

66 99

When it comes to hostels in Colombia, you really need to read customer reviews carefully.

Cartagena

Airbnb and house rentals

Airbnb has become so popular that even the smaller cities of Colombia have plenty of options available.

Be aware though, as many Airbnb options in Colombia tend to let out individual bedrooms – private bathrooms may or may not be included.

If you're willing to spend a little more, fully-furnished apartments are also available. Be sure to check with hostels too – they sometimes offer long-term *apartastudios*, or studio apartments, at lower rates.

Camping in Colombia

Along the Caribbean coast and Punto de Gallo, the northernmost tip of South America, there are some popular camping options available.

Rent a hammock on the beach, take a boat out to an island and stay in a cabin, or go on a three to four-day hike to La Ciudad Perdida, or the Lost City, and experience jungle trekking at its finest.

In the Central Andes Mountains, Los Llanos (Eastern Prairies), and the coastal jungles, you'll find lots of national parks perfect for hiking trips.

Camp grounds are available in many of these areas, but be sure to take care of your belongings, and always check to see if the area you intend on visiting is safe for travelers.

Gregg Bleakney
Cartagena

Getting Around

Despite having no train system, transport in Colombia is surprisingly efficient. All major cities have at least two mass transit options and the latest addition – Uber – means getting around is easier than ever.

Cartagena

Buses

Buses are probably the most widely-used and, in many areas, a safe form of transport in Colombia. In most cities, you can stop any bus that passes, including regional buses. Just wave and be ready to pay when you board.

Be aware though, certain bus routes and stations in the large cities can put you at risk of theft or robbery, so check the local blogs and forums for the latest safety information.

For female travelers, try to sit on aisle seats to prevent getting cornered and harassed. This doesn't commonly happen, but if it does, sitting there will put you in front of more witnesses in

Bogota

> " For female travelers, try to sit on aisle seats to prevent getting cornered and harassed.

case someone tries to bother you.

Local tip: Look out for the local *buseta*, or minivan service. These double up on some common commuter routes and because they're smaller, especially along the route from Pereira to Medellin, they can cut up to an hour off the standard travel time.

Mass transit systems

In major cities, the mass transit system is the main way locals commute day-to-day. Bogota boasts the Transmilenio, Cali the Mio, and Medellin has the Metro, the only commuter rail line in Colombia. These are generally safe for travelers, easy to navigate, and provides access to the main tourist sites and neighbourhoods.

Taxis

You'll find taxis in all cities and small towns in Colombia. Some places, like Tulua, may even offer bicycle taxis.

Bogota

Rural regions might have motorcycle taxis and boat taxies, but try to avoid the moto-taxi. These three-seater tuk-tuks can be quite dangerous, with high accident and mortality rates.

Always try to remember the taxi number in case you leave anything behind. Some of the larger cities, like Bogota, have had fake taxis pick up travelers and then leave them without their belongings.

Never get in a taxi with license plates that don't coincide with the city you're in. For example, in Bogota, all license plates will say "Bogota" on the bottom.

Local tip: In Medellin, check with local hotels for shuttle options from the airport, as taxis tend to be quite pricey, even for Colombia.

Air travel

One of the most cost-effective ways to travel in Colombia is by plane. There are a few national carriers that offer very low rates if you book ahead of time.

A round-trip, like the one from Pereira to Bogota, can cost US $50 if you plan at least two weeks ahead of the arrival date.

However, this doesn't come without

risk, as these same "cheap" airlines have suffered some bad PR in the last few months due to fuel shortages and maintenance issues.

For domestic flights, plan to arrive at the airport at least 45min to an hour before your departure time. For international flights, you must be there two hours prior.

Rules have become stricter over the last couple of years, along with lower weight limits for baggage. Check with your airline prior to travel to ensure there are no surprises waiting for you.

Boats

Some locations in Colombia can only be reached by boat, like Nuqui and Providencia Island on the Caribbean coast.

Boats are infrequent though, so make sure you check the schedule ahead of time to ensure you have a way to get there, and that it coincides with your check-in times.

Talk to your hotel about shuttle options when you make your reservation and ask around to make sure your boat company is reputable.

SIM cards and WhatsApp

SIM cards and phone contracts are readily available. Prepaid cards cost as little as COL$5,000 (US$1.70) and can be topped up monthly with anything from COL$5,000 to COL$50,000, depending on personal usage.

There are three main mobile service providers in Colombia: Claro, Movistar, and Tigo. Each offers different services and network coverage.

The majority of mobile providers, whether prepaid or contract, offer Whatsapp, Facebook, or Twitter – for free – with unlimited usage for the length of the plan.

In Colombia, it's not popular for people to text each other because it's expensive, so everyone uses WhatsApp as a messaging service – even businesses and delivery services use WhatsApp.

Colombian Cuisine

Colombian cuisine is extremely diverse, with each region boiling, frying, grilling, and baking according to distinct preferences and traditions. From hearty soups to fresh tropical fruits, get ready to be dazzled by this kaleidoscopic national menu.

Bogotá

Main dishes

If you love hearty, meat-filled soups and dishes, Colombia will not disappoint.

Try the national dish: *bandeja paisa*. It's essentially a tray of meat with red beans, avocado, fried plantains, a fried egg, chorizo, rice, and an *arepa* – flat cornbread fundamental to any Colombian meal.

If you're feeling adventurous, try *sopa de mondongo*, a delicious soup made predominately with tripe. Otherwise, *sancocho*, a stew of potatoes, yucca, corn, plantains, and either fish or meat, is another popular dish that is adapted throughout the country according to local taste.

In the high Andean region, *ajiaco* is a must-try chicken and potato soup.

For relief from a big night out, a bowl of beefy *caldo de costilla* will sort you out.

Another Andean favorite is the unusual – yet tasty – *changua* soup, made with milk, eggs, cilantro, and pieces of stale bread.

Along the Caribbean coast, locals in Santa Marta traditionally start their day with *cayeye* – mashed boiled green bananas with grated cheese and *hogao*, a tomato and onion relish.

A coastal lunch includes fried fish, *patacones* (flattened fried green plantains), and *arroz de coco* (coconut rice).

Snacks and street food

Empanadas (fried turnovers stuffed with meat, cheese, or vegetables), *pandebonos* (small, cheesy, corn flour and yuca buns), and *buñuelos* (fried balls of cheesy corn dough) are just some of Colombia's favorite snacks.

For a delicious, not-so-healthy option, *arepa de huevo* (a deep-fried arepa filled with an egg) is popular along the Caribbean coast, and it won't disappoint.

A much healthier option is a *tamal*, a

Chocolate Breakfast?

In Colombia, chocolate is prepared as a hot breakfast drink with panela, or bricks of sugar, that melt in hot water. It's served in a special pot with a slight neck called an *olleta*.

Once the panela melts, the chocolate is added and then stirred with a *bolonillo* – a special stick with a wooden ball on the end – designed to break up the chocolate.

Often, milk is added either in place of the water or as an extra addition to help cool it faster.

flavorsome mix of cooked corn dough stuffed with meat, potatoes, and vegetables, all wrapped in a banana leaf.

Be adventurous and try *hormigas culonas*: roasted or fried "big-bottomed ants" – a rare delicacy in Santander.

Marranitas, fried green plantains stuffed with *chicharrones* (fried pork belly), are a popular snack on the Pacific coast. As are *aborrajados*, deep fried battered plantains sandwiched between grated cheese and guava paste. Heaven!

Drinks

Colombia is the mecca of tropical fruit, and fresh fruit juice can be found on every street corner.

The Pacific coast has some fantastic fruit combinations. Try a *cholao*: an icy slush of fresh fruit, drenched in flavored syrups and sweetened condensed milk, and topped with cherries and shredded coconut.

For less of a sugar-high, sip on a *lulada*: an icy drink of lulo and lime juice.

The fermented *champus* (a traditional, regional drink made with corn, pineapple, lulo, cinnamon, cloves, and orange tree leaves) is definitely an acquired taste.

Treat those cold Bogota mornings or hot coastal afternoons with a cup of hot or cold *aguapanela*: a drink made from hardened unrefined sugar cane juice. Lemon or lime is often added.

Take care with Colombia's national drink, *aguardiente*, an anise-flavored

❝❞

Colombia is the mecca of tropical fruit, and fresh fruit juice can be found on every street corner.

spirit derived from the distillation of sugar cane. It means "fire water", and you may need a large *caldo de costilla* afterward.

Desserts and sweets

Colombians love sweet things. *Obleas*, two disc-shaped wafer cookies sandwiched between *arequipe* (a creamy caramel spread), condensed milk, chocolate, raspberry jam, cheese, or coconut, are sold in plazas and street corners around the country.

Other favorites include *salpicón de frutas* (chopped fruit mixed with *Colombiana* soda and a dollop of ice-cream), *cocadas blanca* (a mix of shredded coconut, sugar, coconut water, and cinnamon), and *bocadillo de guayaba* (a sweet block of guava pulp and *panela*).

Ordering Coffee, the Colombian Way

In the Colombian *campo*, or rural areas, hand-roasted ground coffee is often prepared by simply boiling the grounds with panela – an unrefined whole cane sugar – in water. This is the tradition of the *cafetero*, or Colombian coffee grower.

For city-folk, the typical coffee preparation is called *tinto*, or black coffee, with two small sugar straws on the side as sweetener. They are small but strong. If you prefer to have coffee with milk, ask for a *pintadito*.

Thanks to globalization, coffee culture is fast evolving in Colombia today. A third wave (known as *tercer ola*) of coffee producers are educating their local communities on how to drink good coffee.

Many are opening their own coffee shops featuring techniques previously known only in obscure, first world coffee niches. So, expect to be able to order your favorite cup of joe as a single-origin, slow-roasted double skim latte within a few years.

Cultural Highlights

Colombia's culture, though heavily influenced by the Spanish colonial era, varies greatly from region to region. That being said, a few things like Roman Catholicism, salsa, and a universal love of football still unites the nation.

Festival de Orquestras

La Ciudad Perdida

Colombia contains a wealth of pre-Hispanic treasures, but it's most famous is undoubtedly Ciudad Perdida.

Founded around 800 AD and rediscovered in 1972, the Lost City is hidden in the jungles of the Sierra Nevada mountains. It's known as Teyuna to local indigenous groups (believed to be the city's founders), and is made up of a series of spectacular terraces carved into the jungle-clad mountains.

As it's only accessible via a steep climb up 1,200 stone steps. Visiting the Lost City requires a demanding, 4 day, 44km (27.3 mile) trek into the jungle and features several river crossings.

San Augustin

San Agustín

According to UNESCO, the San Agustín Archaeological Park is South America's largest collection of religious monuments and megaliths. Left behind by a mysterious Andean culture between the 1st and 8th centuries, the stone figures depict gods and animals in a variety of styles, depending on the age of the statues.

There are enough sites here to keep you busy for a few days. You can buy a 'passport', which gives access to all of the sites, including Alto de los Ídolos and Alto de las Piedras in nearby Isnos.

Other pre-Hispanic sites

In Bogota, don't miss the Museo del Oro. With over 6,000 pieces on display, it's the most important repository of

6699
You can buy a 'passport', which gives access to all of the sites of San Agustin, including Alto de los Ídolos and Alto de las Piedras.

pre-Hispanic artifacts in Colombia. It also contains the iconic Muisca golden raft, which depicts an indigenous ceremony that formed the basis of the legend of El Dorado.

Outside Bogota, you can visit Guatavita Lake – a sacred site for the Muisca people where the raft was found.

One of Colombia's most spectacular – and rarely visited – pre-Hispanic archaeological sites are the ancient cave paintings found around the jungles of Guaviare department. These beautiful, blood-red images were painted nearly 10,000 years ago. The main sites here are Cerro Azul and Nuevo Tolima.

Colombia's colonial towns

With immaculately preserved architecture, fascinating history, and evocative places to stay and dine, a visit to Colombia's colonial towns are a must on your itinerary.

Barichara, just outside of San Gil, is a perennial favorite. Founded in 1705 on the site of a Virgin Mary apparition, the town is known for its beautiful climate, upscale charms, and handsome sandstone architecture plucked straight from a telenovela.

Mompox, with its UNESCO-protected streets, also wears its cultural legacy with pride. Despite its sometimes-scorching climate, it's popular with travelers and photographers, as it looks much the same today as it did in the days of Cervantes.

Some 132km from Cali, Popoyan is one of Colombia's best-preserved colonial towns. This spirited university town has the nickname "White City" – a nod to its signature white-on-white colonial buildings.

If you're spending more than a day here, don't miss the chance to explore the rugged mountains nearby, filled with thermal waters, waterfalls, and challenging hikes to the crater of Volcán Puracé.

Salsa

Music and dance are a huge part of Colombian culture, so no trip will be complete without a night out dancing to salsa, *vallenato, reggaeton, cumbia,* or *champeta*. Whether it's a pumping nightclub in Bogota, a beach bar, or a *tienda*, the music (and rhythm) is gonna get you.

Don't miss the chance to watch live performances of Colombian musicians such as Carlos Vives, ChocQuibTown, Bazurto All Stars, or Systema Solar. They will rock your socks off.

Witness the true musical culture and heritage of the Colombian Caribbean coast at the Barranquilla Carnival. Usually held in February, this four-day festival shows visitors the real passion and dedication that the local *costeños*

Tejo: A Traditional Game

Tejo is a traditional Colombian team game that's often referred to as Colombia's national sport.

It's played in a large, warehouse-style building divided into 4 or 5 tejo fields.

Each field is 19.5m (64ft) long and 2.5m (8.2ft) wide. At each end of the field, there's a wooden, clay-filled box, set at 45 degrees, measuring 90cm (35 in) wide and 1m (40 in) long.

In the middle of the box, just under the surface of the clay, is a hollow pipe filled with gunpowder.

Each player has a metal puck (a "tejo") and the object of the game is to throw the puck at the clay, and hit as close to the circular pipe as possible. Points are awarded for the tejo hitting inside the circle or the closest to it.

If the tejo hits pipe, the gunpowder explodes, firework style.

Tejo courts only charge for a crate of beer for you to enjoy while playing.

have towards their traditions…and a good party.

For a non-stop celebration, head to La Feria de Cali, where salsa fever is the number one illness in December. For five days, the city turns into an extravagance of live shows, street parties, and dance championships.

For more of an African vibe, the Petronio Alvarez Festival, held in Cali every August, is sure to get your feet stomping.

Football fever

Red or yellow t-shirts, people leaving work early, shops closing early… these are all signs that Colombia is going to play a soccer match.

As a national favorite pastime, soccer unites Colombians. When you hear *"Goooooooooooooooooool!"*, you'll know that Colombia has gained a higher position on the "world's happiest

> For a non-stop celebration, head to La Feria de Cali, where salsa fever is the number one illness in December.

Gold Museum, Bogota

Gregg Bleakney

countries" ranking.

The largest stadium is El Metropolitano in Barranquilla, and is the home ground of the national soccer team. Don't miss a chance to experience the electric energy of a match here.

Influential artists

Colombia's most famous artist is Fernando Botero; a figurative artist and sculptor from Medellin.

His exaggerated and voluptuous sculptures and still-life paintings led to the creation of the "Boterismo" style.

His work can be seen in the Botero Plaza and the Museum of Antioquia in Medellin, as well the Botero Museum in Bogota.

If you're a fan of literature, don't miss a trip to Aracataca. This is the hometown of Gabriel García Márquez, nobel prize-winning author of *A Hundred Years of Solitude* and *Love in the Time of Cholera*, among others.

Traveling throughout Colombia, it's easy to notice how easily the line between fact and fiction is frequently blurred within his works.

Cartagena

017

Safety & Kidnapping

Crimes such as muggings, pickpocketing, and cell phone theft are unfortunately common in Colombia. But with a few insider tips and a big dose of common sense, there's no reason to miss out on this enchanting country.

Peace and travel today

Colombia's violent reputation was born of 52 years of brutal civil war. More than 220,000 lives were lost and around six million people displaced.

The Marxist rebel group, FARC, murdered indiscriminately, recruited children as soldiers, and ran drug, kidnapping, and extortion rackets to fund their cause.

When paramilitary militias, formed by rich farmers and cattlemen, mobilized against the FARC, the rebels made a retreat to remote jungles and southern border zones. Although right-wing paramilitary groups also committed atrocities during the half-century of bloodshed, public opinion largely holds the FARC accountable.

Following four years of intense negotiations in Havana, President Juan Manuel Santos (who notched up a Nobel Peace Prize for his efforts) and FARC negotiators finalized a deal in August 2016. The initial deal was knocked back after a national vote, but on November 2016, a modified deal was finally passed.

Today, tourism in Colombia has grown

Ciudad Bolívar

by over 260% since 2002. Overall, travel to Colombia increased nearly 10% in 2015 alone, and according to the US Department of Commerce, 80% were for leisure rather than business purposes.

Traveler safety in Colombia

In February 2010, the French government declared parts of Colombia to be "safe": adding Santa Marta, Barranquilla, Bogota, Tunja, Bucaramanga, as well as the Zona Cafetera departments of Quindio, Risaralda, and Caldas to Cartagena and San Andres as destinations approved for travel.

Travelers who've actually been there overwhelmingly rave about the place. Many say it's more beautiful and safer than other South American countries, as long as you stick to the popular tourist destinations.

This seems to be the key: going off the beaten path might not be the best idea in Colombia, and when you're in the big cities, ask locals or other travelers which areas to avoid.

Will I get kidnapped?

The historic peace agreement, together

“”
Going off the beaten path might not be the best idea in Colombia, and when you're in the big cities, ask locals or other travelers which areas to avoid.

Craig Blackley

with increased security forces in cities and along major roads, have led to a significant decrease in kidnappings. In fact, kidnappings have fallen a whopping 92% since 2000.

Although there is an agreement with the FARC, there are other groups that continue to pose a risk in certain areas of the country. It's a good idea to research government warnings to ensure that you're not putting yourself at risk.

Departments, excluding their respective capital cities, which should be avoided according to several governments, include Nariño (except the Ipiales border crossing), Putumayo, Arauca, Cauca (except the road between San Agustin ruins in Huila and Popayan), Caquetá, Guaviare, Guainía, Vichada, Huila, Norte de Santander, Santander, Chocó (except the whale-watching towns of Nuquí, Bahía Solano, and Capurganá).

It's also recommended to avoid rural areas in northern Antioquia, southern Cordoba, southern Valle de Cauca, and southern Bolivar. With the exception of Villavicencio and Caño Cristales, the department of Meta should be completely avoided.

The Venezuelan government has temporarily closed its land borders with Colombia due to security concerns and the smuggling of contraband. Check with authorities for the latest security updates before traveling near the border.

Taking buses and public transport in Colombia is safe, and there is a very, very slim chance of being kidnapped.

However, try to always travel long distances during the day and with a reputable bus company, such as Marsol, Berlinas, Expreso Brasilia, or Rapido Ochoa. These companies always travel on main routes, only stopping to pick up passengers at official bus stations.

Express kidnappings: Paseo Millonario

The so-called *paseo millonario* (millionaire's ride) happens when criminals, working with taxi drivers, take a passenger to various ATMs and force the victim to withdraw money.

The abduction doesn't last long (24-48h) and victims are released unharmed. The targets are usually middle-to-wealthy Colombians, as well as foreign tourists for their perceived wealth.

Although this type of crime doesn't happen often, it's important to be aware that criminals are opportunists – by avoiding vulnerable situations, this will not happen to you.

Never flag a taxi from the street, especially in dodgy or tourist areas in big cities, or if you are alone. Always call a taxi from a restaurant, bar, or hotel, or use a mobile app such as Tappsi or Easy Taxi. Never use taxis with a driver and somebody else inside, which is a common

8 Quick Safety Tips for Colombia

- Try to keep a low profile.
- Don't flash your money or valuables.
- Don't use illegal taxis.
- Buses can be a problem, as are rural roads where a single car is an easy target.
- Don't drive on rural roads at night at all.
- Lock the doors of the car, and keep at least half a tank of fuel.
- Roll the car windows up, especially during traffic jams, as criminals are known to snatch belongings while you're in the car.
- Don't travel alone.
- Watch out for drink spiking at bars and clubs.

robbery tactic.

Leave bank cards, passport, and valuable jewelry locked up in the hotel safe and only carry a copy of your passport and enough money for the day/night. Alternatively, bring a credit card with a low limit.

Solo female travel safety

It's perfectly safe for solo female travelers to visit Colombia. However, as a foreigner, you might find yourself in vulnerable situations. To stay safe, be aware of your surroundings and always know your limits. Never accept drinks from a stranger or leave your drink unattended.

Women may also find that they receive quite a bit of attention from Colombian men. Most of the time, it's just harmless flirting and you don't need to worry. Nevertheless, take precaution (and a

> **Leave bank cards, passport, and valuable jewelry locked up in the hotel safe and only carry a copy of your passport and enough money for the day/night.**

touch of skepticism) when approached by a stranger, especially in bars and nightclubs. If you're not interested, don't be too friendly.

Learn a few Spanish phrases to reject any unwanted advances – it can help you get out of an uncomfortable situation. For example,"*gracias, pero estoy esperando a mis amigos*" means "thank you, but I am waiting for my friends". "*Gracias, pero no estoy interesada*" means "sorry, but I am not interested".

LGBT travel in Colombia

Even though homosexuality is not against the law, intolerance and discrimination have been reported – especially in rural areas of Colombia.

With this in mind, when traveling to smaller towns and rural areas, use discretion and avoid public displays of affection.

Don't place yourself in vulnerable or risky situations. When you arrive at a new destination, ask what the attitude is towards homosexuality in a new town or area.

Medellin is an extremely diverse city, and every June it hosts the annual Pride Parade, demonstrating the city's support and its progression towards being a gay-friendly city.

Bogota is home to Theatron, the biggest gay nightclub in Latin America. It's also home to more than 70 nightclubs, 50 bars and restaurants, 11 travel agents and beauty salons, and 7 accommodation facilities – all deemed as LGBT+ safe spaces in order to show the city's openness, acceptance, and tolerance towards the community.

Ayahuasca

Going into a jungle to drink an ancient concoction to spiritually cleanse your mind and body sounds adventurous, right?

With several deaths surrounding an *ayahuasca* ceremony, there are a few things to consider before taking part.

Known as *Yajé* in Colombia, *ayahuasca* is an infusion of several plants that have been used for centuries by South America's indigenous people for healing purposes.

Ayahuasca is not a recreational drug, as it has exceptionally powerful hallucinogenic properties: people with pre-existing health conditions may have fatal reactions to it.

Participants, especially women, are extremely vulnerable during their "trip" to sexual assault and rape. Since there is no control over this type of activity, self-proclaimed "shamans" are suddenly appearing, luring tourists into expensive retreats, and administering potentially lethal doses of the potent tea.

If you do choose to participate in an *ayahuasca* ceremony, be sure that you have done your homework to avoid placing your life into the hands of a phony.

Visas and Vaccinations

It's one of those ever-present tasks that drive us all nuts, but it's important to make sure your paperwork and health checks are in order before stepping foot in South America. Here's what you need to know to make sure your trip is worry-free.

Visas

Tourist visas: For most people, traveling to Colombia is seamless. At the immigration desk, they'll stamp your passport and send you on your way. If you're a Canadian resident, you'll need to pay a fee. Maximum stay for tourists is 180 days, once per calendar year.

Work visas and student visas: One of the most common visas in Colombia is the work visa and study visa. Colombia's working visa is one of the easiest to obtain in Latin America. The most common form of foreign employment is teaching English, but this can apply for many other disciplines too. The process is pretty straightforward. The most common method is to enter the country on a tourist visa, find a job, and then make the border run to switch it over.

Artist and sport visas: It's not uncommon to find "buskers" or traveling musicians in Colombia from other countries. Special visas are available for people who play music, practice an art, or even play a sport.

Cartagena

Typically, these visas can be approved for up to two years.

Vaccinations

Though nobody has ever been asked for a proof-of-vaccine when entering the country, at a minimum, you should be vaccinated for Hepatitis A, Tetanus, and Yellow Fever. If you're going to the Amazon or parts of Chocó, it might be wise to plan ahead, as the airports may ask for your verification upon arrival.

Mosquito-borne illnesses in Colombia

Mosquito-borne illnesses Dengue, Chikungunya, and Zika are present in Colombia.

There are no vaccinations for these. To stay safe and protect yourself from being bitten by an infected mosquito, make sure you apply repellent religiously, wear long pants and long sleeves at dusk and dawn, and sleep under mosquito nets in high-risk areas.

Always remember mosquitos are especially active in low altitude regions. Check for any updates before you travel to a possibly-infected area.

> Colombia's working visa is one of the easiest to obtain in Latin America.

BOGOTA
and Surrounds

Colombia's most cosmopolitan city is a mix of old and new, local and international. From pre-Hispanic historical centers to hipster bars, Bogota is ready to take its place as a world-class travel destination.

Must See and Do

La Candelaria

Take a walk along the narrow streets of Bogota's historical center, home to many museums and fascinating sights.

Don't miss the famous Gold Museum. A large collection of pre-Hispanic artifacts, gold, and metal works are on display here, and the exhibits are expertly curated to take you on an informative trip through Colombia's ancient cultures.

Also a must-see is Bogota's most popular art museum, the Botero Museum. The exaggerated "Boterismo" works of accomplished Colombian artist Fernando Botero, along with Dalí and Picasso, are on display here.

On the way to admire the colonial architecture of Plaza de Bolívar – surrounded by the Palace of Justice and the Cathedral of Bogota – stop off at the city's oldest cafe, La Falsa Puerta for hot chocolate and cheese.

Give the local ritual a try: throw the cheese into your hot chocolate and scoop up the resulting melted goodness with a spoon. It's surprisingly delicious.

Colpatria Tower and Cerro de Monserrate

To comprehend this massive, sprawling city from above, there are two options.

The cheapest and easiest way is to reach the top floor of the Colpatria Tower – a 50-floor skyscraper that offers panoramic views of the metropolis.

Santa Fe

For spectacular views of not only the city, but the surrounding mountains too, take the cable car up to Cerro de Monserrate, which sits at 3,152m (10,340ft). Arrive just before sunset to enjoy the evening sky as night takes over.

While you're here, stop in at Casa Santa Clara – a restaurant specializing in typical Colombian food and drinks.

José Celestino Mutis Botanical Garden

Escape the chaotic streets of Bogota and take an easy stroll to observe flora unique to the Colombian Andes, Amazon, and the Guajira desert in the José Celestino Mutis Botanical Garden.

With a collection of more than 19,000 plants from all over Colombia, the garden is the country's largest botanical garden and acts as both a recreational green space and a research center.

> " For spectacular views of not only the city, but the surrounding mountains too, take the cable car up to Cerro de Monserrate.

Usaquén

In the north of the city lies the colonial neighborhood of Usaquén. The wonderfully preserved buildings are now full of restaurants, cafes, and bars, offering a wide range of national and international cuisine.

Every Sunday, Usaquén hosts a flea market, filling the streets with dozens of stalls selling handmade arts and crafts.

Chapinero and Zona Rosa

For a chance to experience the trendy side of Bogota, hang out in the neighborhoods of Chapinero and Zona Rosa, where glam meets hipster in a very stylish way. The area is overflowing with pubs, cafes, restaurants, and shopping centers.

Plaza de Mercado Paloquemado

As the meeting point for all Colombian produce, a visit to Bogota's largest market provides an authentic Colombian culinary experience. It's a definite must for foodies. Bring along small notes and coins, and spend a couple of hours trying fresh tropical fruits that can only

La Candelaria

Boyaca

be found in Colombia, snack on street food, and inhale the fragrances of thousands of different flowers.

Septima challenge

For a chance to get intimate with Bogota and to connect and socialize with locals in a crazy cultural scavenger hunt, sign up for the Sunday Septima Challenge, organized by Bogota-based tour agency, Bogotá & Beyond.

Teams of four to five are given a list of fun challenges to complete within three hours along Carrera 7, which is closed to cars on Sundays.

These tasks may include taking a photo of a dog in a Colombian football jersey, a video of a teammate dancing salsa with a local, or of a couple kissing.

Bogota graffiti tour

Discover Bogota's vibrant street-art scene and the culture surrounding it. The walking tour is led by local artists who'll share with you the stories behind these powerful murals, as well as interesting insights into the politics and the history of graffiti in Bogota.

Getting Around Bogota

TransMilenio
There's no metro in Bogota, but this bus rapid transit system covers several routes along main roads. It's the fastest way to escape heavy traffic. Avoid it during rush hour though, as it gets extremely crowded. And always beware of thieves.

SITP buses
SITP and TransMilenio are the cheapest options. Buy a Tullave card if you plan to use both systems and download the Moovit and TransmiSitp apps for costs, stops, and routes. Make sure you top up your card in advance for SITP.

Taxis
Taxis in Bogota are not very expensive. For safety, don't hail a taxi on the street – use apps or call (or ask the restaurant/hotel/club) to book.

Uber
This is one of the best and safest ways to get around, although it still faces legal regulation challenges. Take UberX or UberPool for cheaper options, UberBlack for a premium service, or UberVan if you're part of a large group.

Outdoor Activities

Beyond the hills of the huge, fast-paced city of Bogota awaits several adventures that'll bring you much closer to the culture and rolling hills of the Andean countryside.

Explore Ciclovía

Every Sunday between 7am-2pm, certain streets of Bogota are transformed into carless roads. Millions of people take the opportunity to hit the streets walking, jogging, cycling, rollerblading, or skateboarding.

Don't be shy! Put on some sneakers, grab a bike, and go discover the city, one pedal at a time.

Ciclovía

Gregg Bleakney

Climb Suesca's Rock

For rock climbers, the 4km (2.5mi) long cliffs at Suesca's Rock provides over 400 different routes. It's suitable for beginners and pros.

The natural cliffs are close to the town of Suesca, and even if you aren't a fan of precariously dangling midair, set up a tent and go for a cool walk along the railway tracks that are shaded by the boulders.

Hike to La Chorrera Waterfall

A mere 40min from Bogota is Colombia's highest waterfall, La Chorrera, at 590m (1,935 ft). The hike takes you past picturesque villages, friendly farmers, and breathtaking views of the green, mountainous countryside.

Rappelling is also available here and it's absolutely breathtaking.

Páramo Matarredonda

Just outside Bogota lies the Matarredonda Ecological Park, with altitudes ranging from 3,290-3,560m (10,800-12,000ft).

After walking two hours along a

Cascada La Chorrera

> **Don't be shy! Put on some sneakers, grab a bike, and go discover the city, one pedal at a time.**

Salt Cathedral of Zipaquirá

❝❞

Hiking up
to Lake
Iguaque is
a vigorous
adventure
that takes
you to
where the
Muisca
indigenous
people
believed
was the
birthplace
of mankind.

ornaments that have been hand-carved into the rock salt.

Walking through the salt tunnels, illuminated with different colored lights, it'll leave you feeling as if you've stepped into a fantasy world.

Santuario de Flora y Fauna, Iguaque

Hiking up to Lake Iguaque is a vigorous adventure that takes you to where the Muisca indigenous people believed was the birthplace of mankind.

The hike begins at an altitude of 2,850m (9,350ft). From here, the 4.6km (2.9mi) hike takes you up to an altitude of 3,650m (11,975 ft). A round trip takes around six to seven hours.

The weather can be very unpredictable, with temperatures ranging between 8-14 °C (46-57 °F), so be prepared.

A fun plan – and to give you time to acclimatize – is to sleep over at the basecamp lodging and wake up early the next day to hike.

Laguna de Guatavita

Colombia is full of myths, so it's not surprising to discover that the Legend of El Dorado originates just 60km (37mi) from Bogota.

Guatavita Lake was sacred to the Muisca tribe. It was used to perform royal initiation ceremonies, including throwing offerings of gold and treasures into the water.

The two-hour tour through the forests up to the lake may inspire you to believe that there really are tons of shiny treasures lying at the bottom.

pre-Colombian path through gorgeous landscapes, passing flora and fauna unique to the páramo ecosystem (a distinct alpine ecosystem found between the forest and snow line in the northern Andes), you'll reach Lake Teusaca.

Relax on the grassy banks, and enjoy the crisp air and peaceful energy that this once-sacred lake emanates.

Salt Cathedral of Zipaquirá

50km (31mi) north of Bogota in Zipaquirá lies the underground Salt Cathedral. This unique place of worship was constructed 180m (590 ft) below the surface within an operational salt mine. It's been in use since the 5th-century BCE by the Muisca Indigenous people.

Described as "a jewel of modern architecture", the underground sanctuary includes crosses and

Nightlife

Bogota nightlife is vivid and diverse, and you'll find entertainment here every day of the week. Whether you're looking for world-class cuisine or the best rumba spots in the country, Bogota has it all.

Nightlife districts in Bogota

The historic center of La Candelaria, a bohemian and artistic quarter, is the preferred destination for visitors looking for entertainment at cheaper prices. However, its relatively empty streets on weekdays means you should take extra safety precautions – especially at night.

Quiebra Canto, where lots of foreigners gather, is a good option for salsa nights or a more eclectic party on Wednesdays.

Locals prefer to head north for more options. Not far from La Candelaria is La Macarena, also known as Zona M.

This area features bars, pubs, cafes, and restaurants with a more

Downtown Bogota

romantic character. The district's cozy and colorful restaurants offer great places for a drink and eating out with someone special.

Zona G is a calm and upscale quarter of gourmet restaurants, located in an exclusive neighborhood.

El Cielo stands out for its unique culinary concept of molecular cuisine, providing a pricey sensorial experience.

The cool atmosphere of bars and cafes like Juan Valdez Orígenes, stylishly decorated with a cozy top-floor terrace, are excellent for a relaxed evening.

Party-lovers should head off to Zona Rosa, the hottest zone for a good local rumba. This large shopping and nightlife sector is surrounded by hotels, chain and high-end shops, all kinds of bars, eateries, and nightclubs.

It's also home to one of the most famous pedestrian areas – Zona T. It's

❝❞ Party-lovers should head off to Zona Rosa, the hottest zone for a good local rumba.

Downtown Bogota

Bogota grafiti tour

perfect for having a nice meal and drinks in one of the sheltered terraces along this T-shaped street.

About eight blocks from there, restaurants, cafes, and pubs encircle Parque de la 93.

Further north is Usaquén, one of the most picturesque neighborhoods in Bogota. It was once an adjoining indigenous town that has preserved its colonial architecture – including narrow, hilly, cobbled streets, a charming plaza, and church.

Usaquén is known for its top international dining, its many pubs, and an art film cinema/bar.

Hottest spots for a fiesta

Don't miss the famous and lively atmosphere of Andres D.C. Each floor of this huge restaurant/club represents hell, earth, purgatory, or heaven. Its eclectic décor includes not only intriguing trinkets, but actors in costumes too.

On Armando Records' top terrace, you can chill out listening to indie, electronic music, DJs, and live music.

If you're looking for something with

> **Perched on top of fancy hotels are modern and trendy bars that serve cool cocktails to delight the senses.**

more local flavor and a little less Taylor Swift, head downstairs to Armando All Stars, where Latin rhythms are waiting to thrill you.

Gaira, owned by the Colombian singer Carlos Vives, is also a local favorite. The live band – hopefully including Carlos himself – and the diverse music are sure to leave you with sore-but-satisfied feet.

Rooftop bars and pubs

Rooftop bars have taken off in recent years. Perched on top of fancy hotels are modern and trendy bars that serve cool cocktails to delight the senses, along with good music and gorgeous views of Bogota.

An incredible number of pubs can also be found all around the city.

Bogotá Beer Company is the biggest chain and The Irish Pub in Zona T is a favorite of locals and travelers.

Usaquén

One Day Itinerary

Cerro de Monserrate

First stop is Bogota's 400-year-old landmark Cerro de Monserrate, via a fun cable car ride.

The spectacular views from this iconic, 3,152m (10,341ft) mountaintop – with a church dedicated to the Fallen Lord – lets you drink in the enormity of this populous city, and see how all its glory fits perfectly between the mountains.

While you're here, pick up some souvenirs at the small market behind the church and sample some of the local food.

La Candelaria st

La Candelaria

When the city disappears behind the clouds, head back down and take the free shuttle to Bogota's historical center, La Candelaria.

This is where Bogota was originally founded – in Plaza Chorro de Quevedo to be exact. It's home to many gorgeous colonial churches (San

> **This is where Bogota was originally founded – in Plaza Chorro de Quevedo to be exact.**

Francisco Church is the oldest) and the city's greatest concentration of museums.

Discover Pre-Colombian cultures at the famous, world-class Gold Museum; art lovers will swoon at the Botero Museum and the Bogota Museum of Modern Art; understand Colombia's national history at the city's oldest and biggest museum, the National Museum; while the Emerald Museum and the stunning Museum of Santa Clara Church tell a fascinating story.

During your exploration, there'll be many opportunities to try street food and snacks – a warm *arepa* or *almojábana* goes well with a hot chocolate or coffee.

La Candelaria

Menú del dia

Lunch is the main meal of a Colombian's day. Most restaurants offer a set *menú del dia* (today's menu) that usually

BOGOTA

Plaza de Bolívar

Gregg Bleakney

includes soup, a main dish, and a drink. A common dish is *ajiaco*, a traditional and delicious chicken and potato soup popular in the Andean region.

Usaquén

Next, take the M82 TransMilenio bus from San Victorino TransMilenio Station north along Septima (Carrera 7), and you'll arrive at Calle 119, the charming colonial neighborhood of Usaquén.

Take a leisurely stroll through the picturesque, narrow streets lined with original colonial houses.

Most of these have been converted into top-notch restaurants, bars, and cafes – so treat yourself to a coffee-and-cake stop here.

Other interesting sights include the Santa Barbara Church and the Hacienda Santa Barbara, which is now a shopping center.

If you happen to pass here on a Sunday, you'll have the opportunity to browse the little stalls of the popular flea market. Anything and everything is sold here: handmade jewelry, paintings, ornaments, health remedies, clothes, as well as food and drinks.

Zona Rosa and Chapinero

Leaving Usaquén behind, walk two blocks to Calle 117. Hop on TransMilenio bus 544B heading south, and get off at Andino Commercial Center in the Zona Rosa.

The Zona Rosa, "pink zone", is located between Calles 79-85 and Carreras 11-15 and is one of Bogota's snazziest districts.

There are dozens of restaurants, pubs, cafes, boutique stores, dance clubs, and shopping malls to help wrap up your day in style and comfort.

South of the Zona Rosa is Chapinero, an expansive area consisting of several diverse neighborhoods.

Foodies can go wild in the exclusive Zona G (Gourmet Zone) district, found between Calle 67-72 and Carrera 3-9, where there are a variety of top-notch restaurants.

> **❝❞**
> There are dozens of restaurants, pubs, cafes, boutique stores, dance clubs, and shopping malls to help wrap up your day in style and comfort.

Usaquén

CALI
and Surrounds

As the "salsa capital of the world", the beat here never stops. Spend the day exploring beautiful churches or hike the surrounding hills. But just when you think it's time for a break, the infectious music begins, and it's time to dance the night away.

Must See and Do

Salsa in Cali

Visiting Cali wouldn't be complete without some salsa dancing – you're certainly spoilt for choice here.

From tiny hole-in-the-wall joints to giant salsa stadiums, the city is overflowing with dance clubs. Don't worry if you're arriving on a weeknight, the beat goes on 24/7.

For a classic, old-school salsa experience, don't miss Zaperoco. As one of the oldest bars in the city, Zaperoco has been the soundtrack to Cali's salsa scene for decades.

La Topa Tolondra is another popular club: it's relaxed, informal, and open virtually every day of the week, making it especially popular with travelers.

Cali locals also rave about the "Lunes de Brisas" salsa event, which takes place every Monday at a large estate outside the city.

More adventurous dancers won't want to miss the Juanchito neighborhood. It's famous for late-

Christo Rey

Battle of the Flowers, Barranquilla

Gregg Bleakney

night salsa parties. It's not necessarily the safest part of town though, so try to visit with a local.

Festivals in Cali

Cali is host to two of Colombia's finest festivals.

The Feria de Cali, which takes place every year from December 25th-30th, is the perfect way to lift those post-Christmas blues. It's one of Colombia's most popular festivals and features street parades, salsa concerts, and exhibitions.

Cali is also home to the fantastic Petronio Alvarez Pacific Music Festival. Held every August, it's essential for anyone who wants to gain a deeper understanding of Colombia's Pacific culture. Local and international musicians converge on Cali during the festival to play traditional Pacific music styles like *currulao* and *bambuco*.

66 99

For a classic, old-school salsa experience, don't miss Zaperoco.

032

La Ermita Church

The city center and San Antonio

Cali's city centre is worth visiting for a couple of hours to enjoy its beautiful churches, parks, and theaters.

The highlight is La Ermita Church, Cali's most recognized building. A stroll around the center should also include a visit to Jorge Isaacs Park, La Merced Church, and Caicedo Square.

Cat-lovers will also want to cross over the river from the park to visit Parque de los Gatos with its 16 giant cat sculptures, including the giant bronze *Gato del Rio*.

The colonial neighborhood of San Antonio is the historical heart of Cali. This is where most of the city's best hotels and restaurants are located.

It's a pleasant area to stroll around on a sunny day, and it's worth walking up to the park on the hill overlooking San Antonio. The view here from the small chapel is one of Cali's most important cultural sites.

Cali's monuments

Cali is home to three spectacular monuments overlooking the city: Cristo Rey, Cerro de las Tres Cruces, and La Estatua de Belalcazar.

The giant Christ statue of Cristo Rey offers spectacular panoramas of the city. Make sure to visit with a group, as the area can be unsafe.

The Hill of the Three Crosses is also a nice hike with a great view: visit on Sundays when security presence is strong, and the locals get their weekend exercise.

The statue of Sebastian de Belalcazar, Cali's founder, overlooks a nice neighborhood, and is more secure than the other two.

Getting Around Cali

Buses

There's no metro in Cali, but the Masivo Integrado de Occidente (Mio) mass transit system runs through 95% of the city in separate lanes. The stations are clean and the carriages are air-conditioned. You can get a Mio card for COL$3,000 (US$1) from many stations. Each trip costs COL$2,000 (US$0.70). Avoid peak times in the morning and evening, as lines can be long.

Taxis

Taxis provide reliable and inexpensive transport. Use the EasyTaxi app to order from the plethora of drivers. Note that the minimum fare is COL$4,200 (US$1.40) and increases slightly after 8pm and Sundays. Take a taxi in groups to ensure safety, especially at night. A taxi from the airport to the bus terminal costs around COL$50,000 (US$16). From there, take a bus or another taxi, which should generally cost no more than COL$6,000 (US$2) to the city center or COL$10,000 (US$3.30) to the south.

Outdoor Activities

Located in the stunning Cauca Valley between the mighty Farallones de Cali Mountain range and the Cauca River, Cali is a great place for nature lovers and those looking for less-touristy outdoor adventures.

Hiking El Cerro de las Tres Cruces

Cali is a mecca for sport enthusiasts, from hiking and trail running, to adventure sports such as rock climbing and mountain biking.

For a refreshing morning hike, walk just one hour up the mountain from the Santa Monica neighborhood to reach El Cerro de las Tres Cruces (Hill of Three Crosses), which offers fabulous views of the city sprawled out below.

Every Sunday, some of the city's roads close and locals hit the streets to walk, run, skate, or cycle.

Pance River

Spend the day splashing in the refreshing waters of the Pance River, which originates high in the Farallones de Cali, or go running, biking, or hiking through the surrounding mountains.

This little gem is 25min from Cali, so avoid the weekends if you want some peace and quiet.

Towards the bottom of the river, you'll find Pance Eco Park, where there

Cali City

> Spend the day splashing in the refreshing waters of the Pance River, which originates high in the Farallones de Cali.

are restaurants and bathrooms.

About 1km (0.6mi) up is the small village of La Voragine, providing similar services, as well as access to the river.

For a "fresher" experience, head about 3.5km (2mi) further up the river to La Chorrera de Indio. Here, you'll encounter a 35m (115 ft) ice-cold waterfall that crashes down into a natural pool.

You can also walk all the way up to Pance Village, where the locals like to bring their pots and pans and make a fire to cook *sancocho*, a chicken and vegetable soup, for a hearty lunch by the river on weekends.

Pico de Loro hike

Within a few hours of hiking into Farallones de Cali National Park, you'll reach Pico de Loro, a mountain peak reaching 2,832m (9,291 ft) above sea level.

San Antonio Church

> **About two hours from Cali, heading towards the Pacific coast, is San Cipriano, a village hidden in the jungle.**

The steep and strenuous hike takes about 3-4h, depending on your fitness levels, but the effort is worth it. The peak has stunning panoramic views of Cali and the rest of the mountain range. Going with a guide is highly recommended.

If you love trail running, sign up for the August North Face Adventure Marathon. It takes runners through the mountains – vertically – for 42/21/16 km (26 /13/10mi).

San Cipriano

About two hours from Cali, heading towards the Pacific coast, is San Cipriano, a village hidden in the jungle.

The beautiful natural environment and clear waters of the San Cipriano River Natural Reserve offer visitors several fun activities to do.

Hire a tube and walk up the river for about 40mins to La Platina, and enjoy the float back down to the village.

There's also a beautiful waterfall nearby. If you're keen to explore this, pause your tube ride at Charco Oscuro and ask a local guide to take you there.

Lake Calima

Enjoy the hot summer afternoons that beat down in the valley at Lake Calima, just two hours from Cali.

The artificial lake is one of the largest in Colombia, and offers many outdoor activities: nature walks, bird watching, horseback riding, kayaking, or just soaking up the stunning scenery in swimming pools and ferry trips.

The continually blowing winds make the lake ideal for extreme water sports. Kite surfing and windsurfing are the local favorites.

With forested mountains rolling into the lake, clear waters glistening in the sunlight, and a huge choice of activities, a trip to Lake Calima is the perfect place to relax and get some vitamin D.

Valle del Cauca

Nightlife

Cali wears the title "salsa capital of the world" with aplomb. Traditional bars brim with passionate locals whose blood pulsates salsa rhythms. Get ready for the party of your life.

Salsa around Cali

Cali offers dance classes, live bands, and expert salsa performances every day of the week. Not many Colombian cities can say this.

Tin Tin Deo's reputation spans the entire country, attracting the finest movers and burgeoning stars. This diminutive second-floor club, its walls emblazoned with salsa icons, comes alive on weekends.

Go on a Thursday night if you can for a discounted entry, and experience a remarkable choreographed dance involving the entire club called *salsa choke*. Come midnight, you'll be glad you came.

Legendary Topa Tolondra specializes in pure salsa, live shows, and professional performances. There's no

need to go with a partner: local dancers like to scour the surrounding tables and pick up newbies. Get there early, especially on "Cool Mondays", as it soon fills up.

"*Loco* (Crazy) Tuesday", usually held at Mazao in Parque del Perro, gives foreigners and locals the chance to mix over a popular language exchange and dance classes, followed by an after party.

Stepping away from tradition, Delirio fuses world-class dancing with circus acts and various themes.

Two giant tents, located in the northern outskirts, host these monthly performances watched by over 1,000 people. And while tickets are not cheap – at around COL$180,000 (US$60) – where else can you witness salsa dancers swinging from trapezes to the beat of Michael Jackson?

Go during the Feria de Cali, the country's major salsa festival held here

> ❝❞
> Stepping away from tradition, Delirio fuses world-class dancing with circus acts and various themes.

in December, for the end-of-the-year extravaganza.

Bars and dining

Keen for a night off salsa? Head to Martyn's Bar. For over 30 years, this American-style rock-and-roll joint has exuded fun. With license plates, flags, vinyl records, and motorbikes dotted around, Martyn's Bar (Wed-Sat) entertains with blaring classic rock music, live bands, and even singing contests.

Alternatively, Mikasa Bar spins out tunes varying from reggae to electro, rock to indie. Transformed from a house, this cozy bar still feels like a friend's wild party as you brush shoulders with the DJ, order drinks over the psychedelic-colored bar, and boogie under palm trees.

Not for the faint-hearted, La Galería Bar is known for its sublime roof terrace, foam parties, and clouds of weed swirling around. Take a look at its salacious décor: Its owner, an artist, specializes in rather graphic sexual paintings, and he isn't afraid to show off his work.

Cali offers great restaurants that serve traditional and international dishes. Some of the best gourmet restaurants you should try include Faro Peñón that serves Mediterranean cuisine, Mister Wings that offers American and Mexican food, and Restaurante Ringlete for traditional Colombian cuisine.

Late-night parties

Just as everything begins to close, Menga, an area in the north, ramps up the party.

Café de Mi Tierra merges salsa, electro, and commercial music to the mixed crowd mingling in the dance area. In its garden, sweating dancers take a breath while groups of friends pass around bottles of rum or *aguardiente* – a must-try, aniseed-flavored liquor.

Still energized? Head to Lolas, a white-domed club whose crossover beats and piercing lasers excite its beautiful clientele every weekend.

Favela also stays open until 6am, thrilling guests with its industrial design, fully equipped with container-style platforms rising above the strobe-illumined dance floor.

> **" "**
> Just as everything begins to close, Menga, an area in the north, ramps up the party.

One Day Itinerary

Cristo Rey

Start the day at the 21m (69 ft) tall statue of Cristo Rey that sits high up on the mountain, overlooking the city. Buy some local snacks and enjoy the stunning view here.

The romantic nature of this spot makes its a favorite for couples, especially in the evening.

Walking up is possible, but don't do it alone, at night, or carrying valuables. It's best to take a taxi here.

Galería Alameda

Next stop is Cali's crazy, colorful outdoor market, Galería Alameda, to get a sense of the city's true vibe.

The market sells everything from weird-looking exotic fruits, vegetables, and flowers, to bizarre meat cuts, love potions, and tons of food stalls.

One specialty here is seafood, so why not try *ceviche* – raw fish or shrimp marinated in a tomato sauce or tangy lime.

Main street, Cali

"

Next stop is Cali's crazy, colorful outdoor market, Galería Alameda, to get a sense of the city's true vibe.

Do try one or two *chontaduros* (with salt and/or honey for extra flavor) – the fastest-selling fruit due its supposed libido-boosting effects – or a refreshing *lulada* made with lulo and lime juice, or a traditional corn-pineapple-lulo-cinnamon *champus*.

Pick up some artisanal souvenirs at La Caleñita too, just outside the market.

A cat park and a river walk

Hop in a taxi and go north less than 3km (2mi) to Museo La Tertulia, Cali's most popular art museum.

The museum also hosts the La Cinemateca movie theatre, which shows independent films from around the world.

Walk to the wide avenue that runs parallel to the river and head to El Parque del Gato de Tejada. Take a selfie with *El Gato del Rio* – a large sculpture of a cat donated by Colombian artist

Christo Rey

Hernando Tejada in 1996.

Since then, several other cat sculptures have been installed, each created by a different artist.

From cat park, walk along the river on the shady boulevard towards the city center.

Poet's Plaza
and Ermita Church

Talk a stroll through Plaza de los Poetas and share some heartfelt rhymes with the statues of poets on display.

Admire the stunning Iglesia Ermita; a 20th-century church boasting European, gothic-style architecture that delightfully contradicts the surrounding modern-day buildings.

Now's a good time to slurp up a *cholao* – a sweet mix of crushed ice, fruit, condensed milk, and flavored syrups, or a *pandebono* – a delicious baked corn flour, yucca, and cheese bun.

National monuments

Pause for a moment on a bench in the palm-filled Plaza de Cayzedo, Cali's main plaza. It's another great place for street food.

La Ermita Church

Pandebono

6699

Try a pandebono - a delicious baked corn flour, yucca, and cheese bun.

Bordering the plaza are several impressive national monuments: the neoclassical-designed San Pedro Cathedral and Palacio Nacional, and the Republication-style Edificio Otero.

Although the center is pretty safe, don't walk south or east from here as the streets become very dodgy in the Sucre and El Calvario neighborhoods.

San Antonio

Walk west 1km (0.6mi) or take a taxi to the historic hillside neighborhood, San Antonio. Considered as Cali's bohemian quarter, this is a great place to grab a coffee and people-watch. In the past, this colorful neighborhood was home to several Colombian writers, artists, philosophers, and musicians.

Walk up to the San Antonio Church, built in 1747, for a great view of the city.

End the busy day with a drink at any of the little bars.

If you're looking for more of a party vibe, cab it to the suburb of Granada, a popular nighttime hangout and one of Cali's best foodie hubs, or head to a local salsa club to feel the true spirit of Cali.

CARTAGENA
and Surrounds

Cartagena de Indias, a UNESCO World Heritage site, is what fairy tales are made of. With a wonderfully preserved Old Town, trendy Barrios and authentic, Afro-Colombian fishing villages, there's plenty to explore in this romantic city.

Must See and Do

Old Town

Old Town is best explored from the Clock Tower, the main entrance to this walled city.

This exquisitely preserved part of town conjures up images of pirates, treasures, and romances initiated between old colonial buildings and along cobbled streets.

Admire the old colonial Spanish architecture and spend some time snacking on street food or grab a coffee at an outdoor cafe.

Highlights here include the large Plaza de la Aduana, Cartagena's oldest plaza, and the Plaza San Pedro Claver.

Nearby is also Cartagena's oldest church, Santo Domingo. It's filled with artisans selling handmade crafts.

Touch the breasts of "the fat Gertrudis", a large bronze sculpture created by Colombian artist Fernando Botero, to bring good luck to your relationships.

At sunset, climb up to the western

Old Town

sea-facing wall for brilliant shots of the sun setting over the Caribbean.

Local tour agency Free Tour Cartagena offers donation-based tours of the Old Town and Getsemaní.

San Felipe castle

Perched on top of San Lázaro hill lies one of the most resilient fortresses the Spanish ever built.

The strategic position of the Castillo San Felipe de Barajas – 40m (131 ft) high overlooking the sea and made with superb military engineering – provided the perfect means to defend the city.

The secret tunnels, cannons, and immense fortifications led to Spain's defeat of the British Vice-Admiral Edward Vernon during his famous attack, leaving South America to speak Spanish, not English.

English audio tours are available and

Getsemaní

❝❞

Touch the breasts of "the fat Gertrudis", a large bronze sculpture created by Colombian artist Fernando Botero.

Old Town

walking in the tunnels is an eerie, yet fascinating, experience.

Getsemaní

Just outside Old Town's walls is Getsemaní. This neighborhood was formerly used to house slaves, but today is a vibrant red light district and Caragena's trendiest *barrio*.

A highlight here is La Plaza de La Trinidad, a popular evening hangout that gets crowded with street vendors, musicians, and locals enjoying the cool night's breeze.

Bocagrande

Considered as the Miami Beach of Cartagena and in stark contrast to Old Town, this long stretch of apartments, restaurants, boutiques, and bars is where the wealthy live, work, and party.

While the beaches aren't as nice as Playa Blanca on Barú Island, or within the Corales del Rosario National Natural Park, they do provide respite from the strong Caribbean sun.

Mercado Bazurto

"Dirty", "vibrant", "authentic cultural experience", "don't go", "go"... these are just some of the conflicting opinions of this local market.

Mercado Bazurto is only for the adventurous and those wanting a glimpse of the other face of Cartagena, far removed from charming streets and shiny skyscrapers.

You'll be able to find anything here from exotic fresh fruit and vegetables, to clothes and electronics. Wear closed shoes and avoid flashing wallets and fancy cameras, as pickpocketing here is a common crime.

Playa Blanca

Spend a glorious day relaxing on Cartagena's most popular beach, Playa Blanca, on Barú Island.

The calm, turquoise-blue water and stunning white sand is perfectly complimented by a massage, fresh fish, and coconut rice.

Reaching the beach is relatively easy, but it's advised to book a tour with a reputable agency to avoid being scammed by bogus tours and exorbitant prices.

Trinidad Plaza

Getting Around Cartagena

Public transport
Cartagena offers a cheap Metrocar service, but it's not recommended for tourists — it's potentially dangerous due to the zones it passes.

Uber
The app gives visitors the convenience of ordering a car wherever and whenever they'd like, and is generally cheaper than taxis.

Yellow taxis
Taxis are quite affordable: Bocagrande to Old City (less than 4km) is approximately US $3-$4. The minimum ride is COL$6,500, which is around US$2. You can also negotiate to hire them for longer trips at an agreed price.

Private cabs
You'll get the best and most comfortable cars, sometimes with English-speaking drivers. Price is arranged with drivers or directly with the cab company.

Bus or mini van
If you're traveling to nearby cities like Barranquilla or Santa Marta, consider a shared bus or mini-van, which offers door-to-door service.

Outdoor Activities

Step outside Cartagena's Old City walls and get a taste of Colombia's fresh air with these five outdoor adventures you must do.

Convento de La Popa

Also known as "La Popa", this 400-plus-year-old monastery sits on top of the highest hill in Cartagena (150m, to be exact).

La Popa grants a holistic view of the city: Cartagena Bay, Bocagrande, La Boquilla, and Old Town can all be seen from the top.

Take a quiet moment to overlook the landscape and appreciate the city's unique topography. Make sure to check out La Virgen de la Candelaria, a statue of the patroness of the city.

Though it's recommended to take a cab up there for safety reasons, the monastery and surrounding gardens are perfect for an afternoon stroll and enjoying the lovely Caribbean weather.

Playa Blanca Beach

> The Rosario Islands' crystalline waters, vibrant sea life, and beautiful coral reefs make it the perfect destination for snorkeling and marine sightseeing.

Snorkeling Rosario Islands

Located just an hour's boat ride from Cartagena's shores is an archipelago of dozens of small private islands. These were once upon a time Pablo Escobar's Caribbean getaway.

The Rosario Islands' crystalline waters, vibrant sea life, and beautiful coral reefs make it the perfect destination for snorkeling and marine sightseeing.

There are also tons of other activities to do nearby, like visiting the Oceanario Aquarium, walking through the interior of Isla Grande (the biggest island), and laying out on sandy white beaches.

Make sure to enjoy a fresh lobster lunch caught by the local fishermen!

Boat tour through Cartagena Bay

There are several places to visit for the perfect Cartagena day trip.

Start by seeing Bocagrande,

Bocagrande Beach

Start by seeing Bocagrande, located between Cartagena Bay and the Caribbean Sea.

located between Cartagena Bay and the Caribbean Sea. This sparkly, commercial neighborhood is laden with glaring white skyscrapers, towering condominiums, shops, art galleries, and long beaches.

Next, stop at San Fernando de Bocachica Castle, a marine fortress on the nearby Tierra Bomba Island, formerly used in defense from pirate raids.

Before heading back to the city, visit the Pueblo of Tierra Bomba, famous for creating the artisanal art that is sold in the streets of Cartagena.

La Boquilla fishing village
A small fishing village located in the outskirts of northern Cartagena, La Boquilla still gives visitors an idea of what parts of the city looked like before the influx of tourism.

Inhabited by Afro-Colombian ethnic groups, La Boquilla remains relatively

untouched.

The beaches are lined with palm-thatched huts serving traditional fish dishes and, if you go around sunrise, fishermen casting their nets into the water and selling their catch.

There are a variety of activities to further explore the village and culture, including canoe tours through mangrove swamps, bird watching, taking a bath in medicinal volcanic mud, watching a traditional dance, and of course, learning about fishing from the locals.

Soak in the mud baths of Totumo Volcano
Just an hour outside of Cartagena is Totumo Volcano. According to legend, this once lava-spewing volcano was tamed by the local priest's holy water, subsiding to the healing mud baths here today.

Spend the day relaxing in the natural, mineral-rich mud while enjoying the beautiful views of Santa Catalina - the crater offers unbeatable, panoramic views - and swim in the nearby lake to clean yourself off before you go.

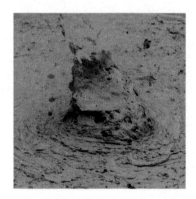

Nightlife

While beautiful by day, Cartagena truly comes alive at night – especially in Old Town – with laughter and music radiating throughout the streets.

Old Town

Local restaurants and dining

Cartagena has some of the best restaurants in Colombia, especially for seafood fans. Stroll down the quaint, cobbled streets of Old Town and you'll have ample options to choose from. Each neighborhood offers a different vibe too, so be sure to explore all the options.

The most romantic and bohemian restaurants can be found in San Diego, while Getsemaní is a young neighborhood with restaurants for all budgets – whether you're dining solo or with a group of friends.

For a livelier night, there are lots of cool dining spots with live music around Plaza de Madrid and Plaza Santo Domingo.

> **Stroll down the quaint, cobbled streets of Old City and you'll have ample options to choose from.**

Latino bars and clubs

Champeta, a genre of folk music and dance with deep African roots, is a must-do after sunset in Cartagena.

The Getsemaní neighborhood boasts plenty of clubs with live Latin music bands, the most famous of them all being the Habana Cafe.

Nearby, visitors can also find the historic club Mister Babilla on Calle del Arsenal, known for its tropical environment and wild nights.

Alquimico bar, a former two-story mansion dating back to 1910, features customized cocktails and a swanky vibe reminiscent of a New York City bar.

Last but not least, those looking to enjoy Cartagena's Caribbean night air can make a visit to Plaza de los Coches, which is full of nightclubs and bars with terraces overlooking the bay of Cartagena.

Bolívar Plaza

Old Town's cobbled alleyways

While Old Town's flower-swathed balconies and pastel Spanish Colonial homes are a delight to see by day, the area has its own charm by night.

The small alleyways are softly lit in the evening, giving them a completely different look and feel. The air here is saturated with Latin music, and the cooler sea breeze offers respite from the hot Caribbean sun.

The walled city can also be explored by horse carriage for those looking to cover more ground.

A walk through Old Town will surely land you in one of the lively plazas. Plaza La Trinidad in the Getsemaní neighborhood, Fernandez de Madrid, and Plaza de Bolivar are the most popular spots where locals and visitors alike hang out after the sun goes down.

> **6699**
> Cartagena hosts festivals all year long, both during the day as well as the evenings.

Battle of the Flowers, Barranquilla

The bay by night

Cartagena's bay can also be enjoyed after hours with a party boat trip. Visitors have the option of renting out a seat or an entire boat.

The average price per person (beverage and food not included) is US $25 and can be directly arranged with the boats by the port.

Larger groups of 10-15 people can directly negotiate with owners to rent the whole boat, as well as arrange catering on board.

Attend a festival

Cartagena hosts festivals all year long, both during the day as well as the evenings.

Storyland, Cartagena's classical and electronic music festivals, are on in January, Colombia's movie festival and "Hay Festival" (a book festival) is in February, and the Miss Colombia contest is in March.

There are also festivals nearby, such as the Carnavales de Barranquilla, which takes place at the end of February and is just an hour's drive north-bound.

Old Town

One Day Itinerary

Holy hills

Start the day with a taxi drive up to Cerro de La Popa, a 150m (492 ft) hill lying to the east of the city.

While the driver waits, spend time appreciating the high-flying views of Cartagena and the Caribbean Sea.

The 400-year old convent, Convento de Nuestra Señora de La Candelaria, is open to the public for a fee.

Explore ancient history at San Felipe Castle

Next stop, colonial Spain's most impressive work of strategic military architecture: the Castillo San Felipe de Barajas.

Skip the guided tours and take a self-guided audio tour of the citadel.

Spend a few hours exploring the complex network of tunnels, admire the impenetrable walls, and the once-powerful cannons.

It gets extremely hot up here, so bring a hat and lots of water.

Experience urban authenticity in Getsemaní

Exiting the castle to your left, take the main road and walk towards Getsemaní.

The once-former slave quarter has transformed into Cartagena's most charming and authentic neighborhood, with dozens of cafes, bars, and hotels.

Take a slow stroll, drink a coffee, and don't miss the fantastic, ever-expanding collection of urban street art that covers the walls of Calle de La Sierpe, creatively illustrating life in this diverse city. If you're into travel or street photography, you'll definitely want to spend some time here.

India Catalina Monument

Leave Getsemaní and walk 10min northeast towards the India Catalina Monument.

The park is dedicated to an indigenous woman, who, after being

❝❞

Take a slow stroll, drink a coffee, and don't miss the fantastic, ever-expanding collection of urban street art that covers the walls of Calle de La Sierpe.

kidnapped by the Spanish, acted as an interpreter and mediator between the Spanish and the local tribes.

Old Town romance

Stop for a selfie at the Clock Tower before you enter the walled city, which will make Gabriel García Márquez fans weep with joy – you can pass his former dwellings, Casa Gabriel García Márquez.

Before getting lost in the maze of colonial alleyways, plazas, and street performances, get energized by buying a couple of typical sweets from the brightly-dressed ladies in the Portal de los Dulces, within the Plaza de los Coches.

Although smaller than her cousin in Bogota, the Museo del Oro Zenú does offer an impressive collection of artifacts from the Zenú indigenous tribe.

Modern contrasts in Bocagrande

Overcome Cartagena's stifling afternoons and rent a bicycle from the bike rental place in Parque Centenario,

Entrance to Old Town

near the Clock Tower.

Head towards the skyscrapers that dominate the skyline of Bocagrande. But beware, traffic can be a little bit crazy, so take care.

As this is the wealthier neighborhood, there are lots of shopping malls, trendy bars and restaurants, and boutique stores to stop at. If shopping isn't for you, a quick dip in the sea to cool off isn't a bad idea, too.

Alternatively, hop on a T103 Transcaribe Bus until Commercial Centre El Pueblito stop.

Tropical sunsets

Ride, or take a bus/taxi, back to Old Town and discover the city from the top of the wide, 17th century walls that were built by African slaves.

Be sure to arrive at the western-facing walls before sunset. Find a spot, buy a beer, and enjoy the sky as it shifts along a color palette.

When night time falls, pick a restaurant within the walls or head to Getsamaní, where La Plaza de La Trinidad is just waking up.

Getsemani

048

MEDELLIN
and Surrounds

As Colombia's most developed city, Medellin has something for every nomad. From innovative architecture and art to wide open green spaces, forget what you think you know about this city of reinvention.

Must See and Do

Pueblito Paisa

Library parks

Dotted throughout Medellin, you'll find several library parks – each with their own style and architectural personality.

The library parks offer visitors the chance to spend time in free internet cafes, read a book, magazine or newspaper, participate in workshops, or just relax outside in the public green spaces.

For great views of Medellin, take a cable car ride via Metrocable to visit the Santo Domingo Savio Library Park, which sits on the eastern mountain slopes.

Built with Spain's support, the library complex has positively changed this poor neighborhood, which was once controlled by dangerous drug cartels.

Parque Arví

From the Santo Domingo Metro stop, buy another ticket and switch to Line L, which'll take you even further up the mountain to Parque Arví. This huge ecological reserve offers several activities including guided hikes through the forests, paddling boats, camping, and the sampling of local food and snacks.

Parque Explora and the botanical gardens

Spend a few hours at the interactive science museum Parque Explora to observe marine life at Latin America's largest freshwater aquarium.

Across the street, you'll find Jardín Botánico, a large green space to sit,

do yoga, or eat salpicon con helado, a Colombian fruit salad with ice cream.

Botero Plaza

Fernando Botero is a figurative artist born in Medellin. He is internationally recognized for his "Boterismo" style, in which he creates exaggerated and voluptuous figures.

As part of an urban revamping program, Botero himself donated 23 bronze sculptures that now make up the Botero Plaza in downtown Medellin.

Besides photographing the crazy statues, you can buy souvenirs or just people-watch while enjoying freshly-cut fruit or ice cream from street vendors.

Museum of Antioquia

Bordering Botero Plaza, you'll find the Museum of Antioquia. The museum displays the work of Colombian artists Fernando Botero and Pedro Nel Gómez,

66 99

Spend a few hours at the interactive science museum Parque Explora to observe marine life at Latin America's largest freshwater aquarium.

Metrocable

Getting Around Medellin

Medellin Metro
The quick and convenient metro cuts through the city from north to south. A single ticket costs COL$ 2,300 (US $0.70), but lines may stretch out of the station, so buy multiple trips. The Metroplus joins the network and has separate lanes on many roads. Stations, which boast user-friendly maps, remain spotless, so no eating or drinking. Some cable car lines, which head up the surrounding mountains, are included in the price.

Taxis
Taxis are cheap and plentiful. The phone app EasyTaxi provides secure rides with registered drivers; the minimum fare is COL$3,000 (US$1). Try to resist taking taxis from the street at night, and travel in pairs or groups.

Buses
The bus network services the entire city. Fares cost about COL$2,000 (US$0.70) and in places where there's no metro, like Laureles and Poblado, buses are useful. Pay cash to the drivers as you get on board.

as well as pre-Hispanic artifacts and contemporary artwork, photographs, sculptures, and international pieces.

If modern art is more your taste, take a peek at the stylish Museum of Modern Art, which hosts new exhibitions every few months.

Pueblito Paisa

On top of the 80m (263 ft) high Nutibara Hill is Pueblito Paisa, a small replica of a typical Antioquian town square. This charming site includes a church, town hall, barbershop, and school. The 360-degree view of Medellin and the surrounding mountains make the visit worthwhile.

You can also enjoy the sculpture park that can be found at the foot of the hill. Open from 6am to midnight, this open-air park showcases several modern abstract sculptures created by national and international artists.

Feria de las Flores

As the "city of eternal spring", it's no surprise that Medellin hosts an annual flowers fair, which promises 10 days of flower and car parades, live concerts, and cultural exhibitions.

Highlights include the famous Silleteros Parade, where people carry large flower displays on their backs in a traditional structure called a *silleta*.

Park of Lights

Outdoor Activities

With a climate that'll make summer-lovers purr, Medellin serves up a wild array of outdoor adventures. From cycling palm-lined streets, to practicing yoga as the sun sets behind the mountains, here are five outdoor activities to explore beyond the city walls.

Guatape Rock

Cycling

There's nothing quite like exploring sun-blushed Medellin on two wheels. Sunday dedicates itself to cycling, with the car-free Ciclovía covering over 30km (18miles) of the city including Avenida Las Vegas and Poblado.

If you're looking for something a little more adventurous, try the tropical ride up Las Palmas or head to the inner city mountain Cerro el Volador, which is buzzing on Sundays.

Every Wednesday night as the sun dips behind the city's surrounding mountain peaks, the SiCLas comes alive.

Medellin

> ❝❞ Every Wednesday night as the sun dips behind the city's surrounding mountain peaks, the SiCLas comes alive.

Meet at 7:30pm at Carlos E. Restrepo to join the peloton of around 1,000 riders, trawling through the city's lesser-visited neighborhoods, passing waving residents, and arriving at some of the finest viewpoints.

Paragliding

Few views bring a wider grin to your face than soaring above Medellin's olive-green mountains and terracotta-colored buildings. Just 40min from downtown is San Pedro, the official takeoff spot.

Go with Paragliding Medellin, who organize private transport or advise on which buses to take. Just be aware: not all travel insurance plans cover paragliding. Check the list of covered adventure sports and activities on our website carefully before you buy your policy.

Pilots take beginners on a 20min

Parque Arvi

Relax in Jardin Botanico

Away from the city's frantic pace, Jardin Botanico allows you to slide into serenity among nature.

Located just outside metro station Universidad, this 14-hectre botanical garden has blooming orchids, swooping butterflies, and roaming iguanas.

On weekends, local lovers deck the grass with picnic blankets, pop wine, and snuggle next to the seductive lake.

A honeycomb-colored indoor space hosts yoga classes (free on Sundays), literary fairs, and concerts.

Visit on the first Sunday of every month to pick up freshly made *tamales*, fresh fruit juices, and locally-grown organic vegetables at the farmers market.

Rio Claro

Three hours from Medellin is this remarkable natural reserve. Voted by Colombians as one of the country's most beautiful rivers, Rio Claro offers rafting, kayaking, swimming, and sailing.

Zip lines also run above the water into the tree canopy, where toucans and monkeys go about their daily business.

The biggest highlight is a venture through the eerie depths of its marble caves. Caving trips require good stamina and swimming capability, with certain parts to be navigated by the aid of a flashlight. Oh, and watch out for those fluorescent scorpions.

Many guests stay overnight in the beautiful wooden cabins overlooking the crystal-clear river.

> ❝❞
> In the Comfama area, a series of zip lines, nets, and ladders take the more daring travelers into the high-altitude tree canopy.

tandem flight in a comfortable harness. If you're keen to get your own flying license, you can even join a course here. It includes theory, practical with an instructor, and solo flights with radio assistance.

Parque Arví

Travel above the sprawling city neighborhoods on the metro cable to reach this ecological playground. As well as forest walks and mountain bike trails, there's a lake for swimming, as well as boating and camping facilities.

In the Comfama area, a series of zip lines, nets, and ladders take the more daring travelers into the high-altitude tree canopy. Groups of 20 or more can explore parts of the area on a new night walk. The four-hour journey ends around a bonfire, drinking wine, and listening to the myths and legends of the land.

Nightlife

It's difficult to keep pace with Medellin's ever-changing nightlife scene. From newly-opened breweries to traditional salsa bars, here's where to get your groove on in Colombia's second-largest city.

Salsa in Medellin

Many bars in Medellin chime to the sound of salsa, and there're few better than El Tibiri. This sultry, low-ceiled basement spot in Laureles attracts the city's finest dancers, leaving crowds of onlookers awestruck.

Lesser-known Cuchitril in Poblado reels in romancers to its vine-shrouded garden area. After 11pm, dancers entwine together in front of live performances.

For those wishing to perfect their dance moves, Santo Baile offers private lessons, while Dancefree spills from the door on Thursday nights during its free (and intensive) group classes.

> **"** One of the major changes to Medellin's nightlife has been the emergence of local breweries.

The burgeoning brewery scene

One of the major changes to Medellin's nightlife has been the emergence of local breweries.

Tres Cordilleras, located in edgy and industrial Barrio Colombia, attracts the crowds on Thursdays for a brewery tour and live rock music. Buy a ticket at the entrance for five beers.

A few blocks away, lesser-known Cervecería Libre (Wed-Sat) serves four house beers, including one passionfruit-infused, and 16 sublime tap tipples best sampled on the taster tray.

In Poblado, Brew House merges a range of international bottled beers and ever-changing drafts with live, televised sporting events. Head there for UFC nights. The owner is a huge fan.

Cocktail bars

The emergence of cocktail bars and electro/house spots has injected class and vigor into Medellin's nightlife.

Alambique, located in Poblado, serves the finest gin and tonics around, as well as exquisite cocktails. Indulge in its array of elegant dishes, especially the tender lamb stew.

Ever since a country house party a few years ago, Breakfast Club has grown in popularity and now leads Medellin's house/electro scene.

Fanatics from all over the country swarm to watch international acts at *Breakfest* events in Parque Norte. Every weekend, Salón Amador reverberates the buildings on La 10, attracting a trendy, good-looking crowd.

Alfresco drinking

Medellin's spring-like climate deems it necessary to hang out in its plethora

6699

At night, lines of food trucks sizzle from frying burgers and billow out scents of sweet-smelling pork.

of parks and plazas.

While Parque Lleras throbs with tourists, Parque Poblado draws an alternative crowd. Groups of friends spread up the rising stairs that encircle the ripped-jeaned musicians, tapping bongos, and strumming acoustic guitars.

Over the last few years, the city's hipsters have swarmed upon Ciudad del Río. At night, lines of food trucks sizzle from frying burgers and billow out scents of sweet-smelling pork.

Locals grab a beer or a salt-rimmed, lime-tinged michelada from street vendors while cocktails and *aguardiente* (aniseed-tasting liquor) appear during live music concerts.

Rooftop bars

Medellin's skyline turns even more magical while mingling with the city's 'it' crowd in a rooftop bar.

Panorama, set among the twinkling palm trees on Provenza, fuses slick modern décor with high-end liquor. Bar staff craft cocktails with the utmost precision, making the high prices bearable. Don't miss the stand-out drink: a sublime sangria.

Nothing says extravagance like a club with a swimming pool and scantly-dressed clientele. Envy, atop Charlee Hotel, entices the who's who of Medellin – soap opera stars included.

Wednesdays welcome live salsa bands and Saturdays bounce with electro DJ sets.

Don't forget to keep an eye out for daytime pool parties.

One Day Itinerary

A walk and coffee in El Poblado

Begin the day with a stroll through the shady streets of El Poblado, Medellin's trendiest neighborhood.

El Poblado is a hotspot for hotels, restaurants, bars, and plenty of places to splurge your pesos in boutique stores.

Savor a fresh brew at one of the chic cafes, and don't forget to buy a bag of single-origin coffee.

Learn about culture in El Centro

Take the Metro Line A to Parque Berrío Station and walk to Plaza Botero.

Here at Medellin's most-visited plaza, you'll be greeted by 23 bronze statues sculpted by Fernando Botero.

On the way, pass through Parque de las Luces and admire the artificial forest of 300 tubes of light. It marks the city's positive change from gangster's paradise to Colombia's most innovative city.

Wander around the Museum of Antioquia and admire the works of both modern and pre-Hispanic artists.

Within walking distance is the gothic-style Rafael Uribe Palacio de la Cultura, which houses an art gallery and historical archives.

Traditional lunch

A typical lunch in Medellin is a rather large endeavor. The famous *bandeja* *paisa* is a tray of rice with an *arepa* (flat corn bread), plantain, avocado, minced meat, chorizo, black sausage, fried pork rind, and a fried egg. It's considered Colombia's national dish. You'll find it at almost every local restaurant serving lunch.

Top it off with a *tinto*, a small cup of sweetened black coffee.

Explore a science museum and botanical garden

By taking Line A north to Universidades Metro Station, we arrive at Jardín Botánico. The 14-hectare garden, its lagoon, and diverse flora and fauna offer a break from the busy streets.

Have some fun at Parque Explora, a large complex with over 300 interactive experiences based on physics, neuroscience, and communication. There's also an aquarium and a

❝❞

Here at Medellin's most-visited plaza, you'll be greeted by 23 bronze statues sculpted by Fernando Botero.

terrarium here if you're more wildlife than science.

Cementerio de San Pedro

Walk less than 1km (0.6 miles) from Parque Explora, to arrive at Cementerio Museo San Pedro, a 19th-century cemetery which has been declared both a national monument and Cultural Heritage of the Nation. Many prominent artists and politicians have been laid to rest here.

Take a walk through the grounds for a cultural experience, bringing life and death, past and present, into one continuous time frame. It's a great way to appreciate Medellin's history.

Santo Domingo Library Park

Line A takes us to Acevedo Metro Station, where you should make a quick switch to Line K, and soar high above the city in the country's only Metrocable.

The Metrocable has changed the lives of the residents living in these poor neighborhoods, safely connecting them with the city.

Exit the cable car at Santo Domingo Metro Station and walk to the large black building: Santo Domingo Savio Library Park. Reach this spot before sunset to enjoy another side of this contemporary city.

Sample Medellin's vibrant nightlife

With tired legs, hop back on the Metro and take Line A south until you're back at El Poblado. End the day with a drink in Parque Lleras, one of the city's most popular nighttime watering holes for ambitious foreigners.

If you're looking for something a little more local, head to La 70, a long strip of bars and clubs in the trendy Laureles neighborhood for a more authentic, Colombian vibe.

> The Metrocable has changed the lives of the residents.

GREATER COLOMBIA

Whether you're looking to explore the sprawling coffee plantations of the Zona Cafetera, or be lulled to sleep on a hammock by the ocean breeze, it's all waiting for you outside Colombia's favorite cities.

The Caribbean Coast

Adventures on Colombia's Caribbean Coast are aplenty. Hike through tropical forests, dive beneath the waves, or just chill on pristine beaches. Get ready to explore a little piece of paradise.

Tayrona National Park

Santa Marta and surrounds

As one of the oldest cities in South America, Santa Marta has a turbulent history full of pirate attacks and legends.

Spend a few days exploring the historical center, drinking fresh fruit juices, and eating in open-air restaurants while street musicians and break-dancers entertain you.

Trek into Tayrona National Park to enjoy sandy beaches surrounded by tropical forests. Take a short trek and visit the ruins of Pueblito, a mini Lost City built by the Tayrona people. You can also go diving and explore the colorful marine life here beneath Tayrona.

Escape the heat and head to Minca, a village just 14km (9mi) from Santa Marta, up in the Sierra Nevada de Santa Marta. This picturesque village has been declared an ecological paradise, and it's famous for its natural biodiversity and organically-grown coffee.

The locals come here to go mountain biking, canyoning, tubing, horse riding, hiking, and splashing in natural pools.

> ❝❞ Trek into Tayrona National Park to enjoy sandy beaches surrounded by tropical forests.

Santa Marta

La Guajira

Palomino, a small village in the department of La Guajira, offers long stretches of quiet beaches, freshwater rivers, and activities like kayaking, surfing, and tubing down Palomino River.

Wake up early to see the snow peaks of the Sierra Nevada de Santa Marta before it disappears into the clouds.

Further along the coast, among the

Johny Cay Island

Learn about the history, identity, and traditions of the Colombian Caribbean at the Caribbean Museum.

"Quien lo vive, es quien lo goza" (Anyone who lives it, enjoys it), is the motto of the Barranquilla Carnival, the second-biggest carnival in the world.

Every year, the city explodes into a magnificent array of music, costumes, performances, and festivities.

For jazz lovers, the annual Barranqui Jazz Festival brings together the best of African and Caribbean rhythms with soul-shaking performances.

For art lovers, the Museum of Modern Art is a great place to check out 20th-century Caribbean contemporary art.

Take a colorful, sensory tour to appreciate the history, music, costumes, masks, and the traditional characters of the famous Barranquilla Carnival at The Carnival House.

dry, seemingly uninhabitable desert landscape, lies the fishing villages Cabo de La Vela and Punta Gallinas – the northernmost point of South America.

Archipelago of San Andrés and Providencia

The cultural mix of Spanish, English, Dutch, and African traditions make this archipelago as diverse as the marine life beneath it.

Spend relaxed days drinking cocktails on white-sand beaches while reggae music sets the tone. Don't miss the chance for some world-class diving, fishing, or snorkeling at El Acuario while you're here.

For a more vigorous adventure, try kayaking, windsurfing, or kitesurfing.

Barranquilla

Barranquilla's rich cultural history is on display at several museums and provides a great understanding to this ever-moving city.

The Romantic Museum is overflowing with colorful Colombian artifacts. Musical instruments and handwritten letters by Simón Bolívar are on display next to the original typewriter Gabriel García Márquez used to type his novel, *Leaf Storm*.

> **The cultural mix of Spanish, English, Dutch, and African traditions make this archipelago as diverse as the marine life beneath it.**

Barranquilla

The Pacific Coast

Colombia's wild Pacific coast stands in stark contrast to the Caribbean. With untamed jungles, hidden beaches, and majestic humpback whales, get to know this once-in-a-lifetime travel experience.

Coquí

Gregg Bleakney

Nuquí

The coastal city of Nuquí is one of the two towns in the Chocó Pacific region with an airport, and is an important gateway to the area for most travelers.

There are some basic hotels and restaurants with 24-hour electricity (rare for this region), but most travelers will want to move on soon after their plane lands.

The nearby beaches of Pico de Loro and Juan Tornillo offer some of Colombia's best surfing, although they are recommended for experts only.

If you're looking to learn to surf, visit Chocó's Club de Surf del Choco (see inset), where you can learn alongside the local community and immerse yourself in the local culture.

Coquí

The community of Coquí, 15min by boat from Nuquí, is home to some of the best-preserved mangrove ecosystems in Colombia.

An eco-guide collective offers mangrove tours of 1-3h in *chingos* – traditional hand-carved canoes.

This Afro-Colombian community has two basic guesthouses, and hosts a gastronomy festival every January and July, offering a window into regional culture.

Guachalito Beach

The most beautiful place to visit is the stunning Guachalito Beach, an hour by boat from Nuquí. This isolated beach, fringed with verdant jungle, has several guesthouses, as well as some of the best humpback whale-watching (from July to October, when the whales visit the Pacific region to give birth), surfing, and ecotourism in the region.

A highlight is El Cantil Ecolodge – beautiful cabins on the edge of the jungle with nature tours and surfing courses.

> ❝❞
> The most beautiful place to visit is the stunning Guachalito Beach, an hour by boat from Nuquí.

061

Bahía Solano and El Valle

The small neighboring communities of Bahía Solano and El Valle are popular travel destinations in the Pacific region. It's excellent for whale-watching.

With plenty of places to stay, these towns also cater for a variety of budgets.

Hop on an hour-long boat trip to Utría National Park, the area's most untouched wilderness.

Here, visitors can hike jungle trails, go bird watching, or relax on Playa Blanca, one of the Pacific's most stunning beaches.

Most whale-watching tours include

> 66 99
> **The waves here are reliable and not too big, and most hostels can arrange surfboard rental and classes.**

a stop in Utría. You can also organize tours to learn about local culture: El Almejal Ecolodge can arrange for an Afro-Pacific musical group to come and perform traditional music. Guides can also learn about Emberá indigenous culture – including weaving, wood-carving, and body painting – from a local family in an authentic *maloka* (cabin).

El Valle's Almejal beach is also an excellent place for novice surfers to get some practice.

The waves here are reliable and not too big, and most hostels can arrange surfboard rental and classes. Lucky surfers can even encounter humpback whales while they 'hang ten!'

Juanchaco and Bahía Malaga

The beachside community of Juanchaco is accessible by boat, just 30min from Buenaventura (three hours by bus from Cali).

Buenaventura is not a particularly desirable place to visit: it's unsafe and unattractive, but you don't have to stay long.

Just head down to the tourist dock and buy a boat ticket to Juanchaco. From there, you can organize return passage to the community of La Plata in Bahía Malaga, where there are also several hotels.

With beaches, waterfalls, diving, and access to Uramba National Park – one of the best whale-watching sites in Colombia – this is the best option for travelers wanting to experience the Pacific coast without the budget for expensive internal flights.

Youth Empowerment & Education on the Pacific coast: Fundación Buen Punto

Nuquí is known by the locals to have "an awesome wave" and stunning natural biodiversity, but you won't see many surfers here.

The remote communities of Termales, Partado, and Arusi, located in the Chocó department of Colombia's Pacific coast, have been heavily affected by the violence and drug trade that have afflicted Colombia.

But a new wave of opportunity, in the form of local surf school *Club de Surf del Chocó*, is set to provide the local Afro-Colombian youths an alternative future and open up the region to adventure tourism.

Thanks to the hard work and donations driven by Fundación Buen Punto, one of our Footprints partners, this local surf school offers access to equipment and classes to 120 young surfers every week.

It teaches the core values of respect, discipline, and tolerance, and a pre-requisite of participation is staying in school and achieving good grades.

For many of the kids, sharing the waves with their friends is the highlight of their week. Moreover, it's given them a way of breaking the cycle, and a new dream of one day becoming champion surfers. The foundation has already sent representatives to the national surfing championships, and the first generation of students are now teachers of the program.

Travelers to the area are invited to get in touch with Fundación Buen Punto to learn to surf alongside the locals – or to just experience the local community and culture.

To learn more, visit https://www.facebook.com/fundacionbuenpunto/

Zona Cafetera

Welcome to Colombia's coffee zone, or *Zona Cafetera*, where a thriving economy serves up some of the best gourmet coffee shops in Colombia, and a big dose of warm hospitality.

The locals of the coffee zone

The central mountain corridor of Colombia is home to one of the most-loved and most-admired cultural demographics, the *Paisas*.

They are the offspring of the *Campesinos*, or peasant farmers of the Colombian Andes, who migrated south during times of political unrest. They also brought the coffee bean to the Zona Cafetera.

This region is most commonly known, inside Colombia, as the Colombian Coffee Axis, or the *Eje Cafetero*. It's made up of three Departments: Quindio, Risaralda, and Caldas. Each has its own unique culture and traditions.

Cocora Valley

Pereira

The legacy of the Paisas

You can see the dominance of Paisa culture everywhere in the Coffee Axis. From their easy humor and warm welcome, they are known as a friendly people.

The men come from farm to city with their ponchos, *carriles* (a type of leather man-bag) and machetes at their sides. The women are famed for their beauty and fashion sense, with light breezy colors and sexy styles. These are also women who are very respected and loved for their passion and warmth. These are the iconic *personajes*, or personalities, of the Coffee Axis.

Their food consists of a few main staples: beans, rice, plantains, corn, and meat or fish. In this region, you can try a favorite cultural dish called the *bandeja paisa*: sausage, ground beef, pork rind, fried egg, beans, avocado, and rice. It comes from a traditional mountain farm

> You can see the dominance of Paisa culture everywhere in the Coffee Axis. From their easy humor and warm welcome, they are known as a friendly people.

diet, which was based on the heavy labor needs of the coffee growers. You can hear their music "*musica parrandera*," in the streets and *cantinas* of the Coffee Zone.

Zona Cafetera

Gregg Bleakney

The capital of the Coffee Axis

The capital of the coffee axis is Pereira. A major crossroads, it's also a very important center of commerce for the coffee region.

Here, you will find a thriving economy with many locally-owned businesses, some of which are very old and well-established.

Discover some of the best gourmet coffee shops in the region, fine dining, and a variety of hotels, hostels, and country villas for rent.

In the outlying areas of Pereira, you'll find bird-watching parks, hiking, mountain biking, camping, waterfalls, and even an exotic garden called Kamala Jardin Exotico.

This garden is home to over 40,000 species of exotic plants, plus an impressive collection of lizards, from around the world.

Come prepared

This region is prone to rain on an almost daily basis. Be sure to bring an umbrella and jacket. Especially in places like Salento, where temperatures will stay cool, it's a good idea to have a jacket and/or long-sleeved shirt and pants with you.

If you travel to the west of Pereira, the climate becomes hotter. For this zone, you'll need bug spray, a hat, and sunblock.

Day trips from Pereira

In every direction of the compass, moving outward from Pereira, you can take short day trips to wander the streets and plazas of historic towns with beautiful architecture.

Whether you're the adventurous type who likes to take a risk and participate in extreme sports, or prefer to explore the botanical gardens and spectacular waterfalls at your own pace, here are a few ideas:

- Hop on a bicycle and then hike to the river and waterfalls of La Florida. Stop off for a lunch of fresh trout from the river on your way in or out.

- In Salento, experience the colonial architecture of the village, then hike up into a protected cloud forest where the endangered Colombian Wax Palms grow. The trailheads are only 15min away by jeep.

- Experience the colorful architecture and artisan crafts of Finlandia, but don't forget to climb the viewing tower for a spectacular view of the surrounding countryside.

- Wander the Casa Paisa Museum and Visitor Center in Marsella, where you will learn how the local culture lived and thrived in the early pioneer days of the coffee zone.

- Be sure to take a day trip up to Manizales, the capital of Caldas. There, you can arrive in the center by cable car, then climb to the very top of a cathedral and see a 360-degree view of the city and surrounding mountains.